The Church and Social Welfare

CHRISTIAN PERSPECTIVES ON SOCIAL PROBLEMS

Gayraud S. Wilmore, *General Editor*

The Church and

and

Social Welfare

by

ALAN KEITH-LUCAS

Philadelphia

THE WESTMINSTER PRESS

Contents

Foreword

THIS BOOK IS ONE OF SEVERAL TO APPEAR DURING the next few years in a series entitled Christian Perspectives on Social Problems. This is an attempt to meet a challenge from an exceedingly robust minority of laymen for brief, readable analyses of cultural problems from a theological perspective. It is intended to help them *think theologically* about some of the exasperatingly difficult problems of society, both the issues which relate to life in America and those which link this nation to the destiny of the world.

Recent researches on family life have found laymen obsessed with "loving, happy relations" in the family, with child-rearing and personal problems of status and adjustment, but with little comprehension of how private troubles bisect public issues. This curious fascination with selfhood to the neglect of neighborhood is not, however, a universal malaise of Protestantism. A minority, perhaps, but a minority that refuses to be lightly regarded by ecclesiastical officialdom, is demanding to know the meaning of events of our day for the Christian faith and to demonstrate the critical and renewing power of faith in secular society.

It is to these doughty men and women that the several volumes of the Christian Perspectives on Social Problems series are directed, and it is hoped that they not only will make for an unsettling reading experience but will provide stimulating material for small-group study and discussion. To that end, questions for discussion are appended to each of the books as starters for fruitful controversy.

The Cleveland Conference on the Churches and Social Welfare, convened in 1955 by the National Council of Churches, marked a historic new impetus in Protestant concern for ecumenical discussion and effort in the social welfare field. In this volume of the Christian Perspectives series Alan Keith-Lucas, a Christian layman and prominent member of the social work profession, points to confusion and error in many Protestant approaches today. He analyzes and raises serious questions about the illusions and pretensions Americans bring to the helping process. This book traces the historical and theological development of social service by the churches and calls for a return to a distinctive Christian realism both for the conduct of the church's institutional program and for its involvement in public welfare policy formation.

In these days when social welfare policy and programs are much in the news, Dr. Keith-Lucas' book will provide the basis for serious study and spirited discussion.

GAYRAUD S. WILMORE

Pittsburgh, Pennsylvania

Acknowledgments

The historical material in Chapter II of this book is based on research done with the help of the Lilly Endowment in the summer of 1958 at Duke University. Chapter VI is based on material previously published as an article, "The Nature of the Helping Process," in *The Christian Scholar* (Vol. XLIII, No. 2, Summer, 1960).

3

Chapter I

Inadequate Answers
to Welfare Problems

MANY AN HONEST CHRISTIAN IS TROUBLED BY THE welfare picture as he sees it in America today. He sees vast, expensive, tax-supported programs, some of which are undoubtedly necessary, but some of which appear to him to maintain people in idleness and some even to put a premium on shiftlessness or immorality. And yet if he knows a family that is receiving aid from the state, he may be appalled that anyone should be asked to live on so little. He fears the bigness of public welfare and the element of Federal control. But when he turns to private agencies, locally supported, he finds himself not free from doubt. He may be aware that private agencies are staffed by professionals who use a jargon he does not understand and who owe allegiance to a philosophy of man very far from that which he considers Christian. He may have met some caseworkers who are frankly opposed to the church and who seem to have little concept of human responsibility. On the other hand, he may know of help that has been given with good results and this may trouble him, making him wonder whether these professionals may not have some skills or values that have escaped him.

If this person is a thinking churchman, he may wonder where the church stands or where it ought to stand on these matters. Is there a Christian point of view on

5

the problems of social welfare? Should the church make its influence felt, and if so, in what direction? Surely the things with which welfare deals—charity, the relationship between the rich and the poor, responsibility, the intervention of the state in details of family living—are things with which a Christian is properly concerned. He may even be aware that for more than a thousand years the church was the primary welfare agency. It alone cared for the sick, the old, the poor, the fatherless, and provided all that now passes for family counseling.

This is not, of course, the picture today. Churches still care for some fatherless children, provide some family counseling, run settlements or homes for unmarried mothers, give a little emergency relief, and of late have with some energy entered the field of care for the aging. There is a national conference on church social work, and many churches have divisions or boards concerned with social welfare. But this is a very minor effort compared with the mass of social services under secular sponsorship. The vast majority of the poor and the troubled turn today not to the church but to the state or to a community-sponsored agency for succor in their distress. Even the church social service committee finds itself more often concerned with steering people to other agencies or providing auxiliary services than it does in being a primary source of help.

What, then, should be the role of the church? Should the church and its members be concerned by what is happening to children in foster homes or those receiving Aid to Dependent Children? Should it be concerned with the quality of justice in the juvenile courts, or the adequacy of Social Security, or the type of counseling in the family service society and the child guidance clinic? Does it have anything to say about the kind of help given to migrants or the running of displaced persons' camps, or adoption laws, or regulations that put a lien on an old person's property before the state will give him aid? Are these purely secular problems, to be settled by ordinary common sense and good will, or are Christian principles involved?

The confusion of the church on these matters is illustrated by the fact that it appears to have given, from time to time and yet continuously, at least seven partial and often contradictory answers. Each betrays an inadequate concept of the church and of its gospel.

The first is the answer of noninvolvement. There are people who believe that social welfare problems are none of the church's business. These are the believers in the pure "spirituality" of the church. To them any specific witness that the church might have in such matters is "intermeddling" in affairs of state. To them the only kind of distress with which the church can be concerned is a man's soul-searching related to his own salvation. The church's only concern with charity is with what each of its members gives to the poor.

As a corrective to the somewhat naïve blundering of some church pronouncements on highly complex matters, there is some virtue in the concept of noninvolvement. It does emphasize that the church has a "different" message. The church is not simply a congregation of men of good will, a sanctified civic club, an ethical society devoted to brotherhood and the proper ordering of society. Its concerns are ultimately spiritual. Yet noninvolvement must be rejected, in its extreme form at least, if only because of that "ultimately." Of all religions Christianity is, in one sense, the least "spiritual." It has never denied the world or drawn a hard and fast distinction between this world and the next. Our Lord himself made it clear that service to others would be accounted service to him, and surely he did not mean that when men act together, as they do in a welfare program, through Congress or the Community Fund, they are any the less accountable for what they do to each other. It is a sad but appalling fact that the church's difference, its being "set apart" to witness to an amazing gospel of love, has been used so often not to transform or illumine the world but to perpetuate its evils and to dull the conscience of the church to the sins of its own members.

2. The second answer is that of opposition to present programs precisely because they are primarily state-supported and professional. These people see the church not indeed as wholly separate and indifferent to what goes on around it but as the last citadel of individual rather than collective action. They object to the welfare picture today, not because of what it does or does not do to help people, but because it no longer allows for the individual impulse of love and charity toward another person.

One can sympathize with these objections. Certainly there is joy in giving, and to give one's love and friendship on a personal basis may mean much more to the recipient than money from some central fund. That this kind of charity may also mean an unwelcome obligation, a sense of subservience, that its primary satisfaction accrues more often to the giver than to the recipient, is not always understood; nor is the fact that professionalism in the welfare field today means a heightening and not a lowering of sensitivity to what others are feeling—a disciplined but not a soulless way of giving. Although there will be always room for personal giving, this is no reason to reject all giving that does not have this immediate quality. Christian stewardship is as important, if not more so, than Christian pity. And those who reject, on Christian grounds, being taxed for welfare purposes, those who would like to return all giving to a voluntary basis, those who see giving through the church as warm and personal and see state programs as cold and soulless, have forgotten an important Christian fact.

This is a fallen world. It cannot rely on the goodness

of even those who profess to be good. The reason why we have today compulsory Social Security, welfare taxes, and a legally established "right to assistance" for those in need is that personal giving has proved in the past to be both inadequate and far too capricious to meet the needs of the people. Personal giving means personal judgment. All too often it has meant giving according to petty loyalties, prejudices, or to satisfy personal whims.

It is true that in the Middle Ages the church rather than the state dispensed what we now know as welfare. But it did not do so to protect the right of the well to do to give as they liked. It could be effective, in that very much simpler world, only because it was large enough, and free, at least in theory, from private interests and factionalism, to present an imperative claim on the hearts and purses of citizens in the name of the dispossessed. It could counteract the tendency of each man to give only to those of his own party or to those whom he approved. The tithe may not have been a tax in the modern sense of the word, but it had, in that age of faith, an authority behind it that very few dared deny. And in Saxon England at least one third of it was dedicated to the poor, which meant that about the same percentage of the national income was spent on welfare as goes to such purposes today.

Today only state and Federal governments have anything like the same authority. They alone can speak for the need of persons of whom private givers do not approve, who are of the wrong caste or color, or have committed the wrong sins—those whose needs are real but unpopular. This is not to say that the actions of the state are always wise, or even that man ought to need governmental programs to ensure that all persons in need get help. But until private giving, or giving through the churches, can come up with a greater equity and a more efficient coverage of need than it has done in the past, the church is in no position to oppose the system as such.

A third, and quite different, answer attempts to testify to the church's concern for those in need. This answer might be called humanitarianism. The church has frequently exhorted its members to be concerned for one another's needs. Yet to be satisfied with this as the church's witness is to have a wholly inadequate concept of what the church is, and says, and does. It is true that the church is humanitarian, that it believes in loving-kindness, that our Lord himself was much concerned with the poor and the sick and with the provision of daily bread. The church may need to remind its members of the duty that God has laid on them. But the church is much more than a center of indiscriminate good will. Humanitarianism, even in the finest sense of the word, is not an exclusive Christian virtue. Indeed in the history of mankind many great humanitarians drew little or nothing from the church, and some were actively opposed to it. Both the Golden Rule and the commandment to love one's neighbor as oneself are pre-Christian. Although Christian love may be their finest expression and Christianity may offer the firmest grounds for their exercise, there is need for a more exact witness. There is need to show how God's promises, his coming down among us, his forgiveness of our sin, have deepened and fulfilled this ethic and what he really means by "loving our neighbor as ourself." There is need, in fact, for a theology of welfare, an understanding of man's mutual obligation in the light of his relationship to God. Otherwise Christianity is of the same nature as Confucianism or the teachings of Aristotle. It is no more than a "right way of life" arrived at without the necessity of God as revealed in Jesus Christ.

An attempt to establish such a theology was made by what is known as the "social gospel." This may be called the fourth answer. The social gospel was a much needed corrective to the "spirituality" of the church, a reaffirmation of God's command to men to practice justice and be concerned with the need of others. It was an emphasis sorely needed at a time when the church was too closely —as it still sometimes is—identified with things as they are: with industrial economics, with the tenets of democracy, with class or cultural interests. But, like so many emphases that come by way of correction, the social gospel took the part for the whole. It remembered a part of Micah's commandment, "to do justice, and to love kindness," but it forgot that he also abjured us "to walk humbly" with our God (Micah 6:8). What it did was to identify God with social justice, and even with particular remedies for the injustices of the time. "The God of lower food prices," says Walter Rauschenbusch in *Christianizing the Social Order,* "He is my God." Better the God of lower food prices than the God of economic exploitation, but neither one is the Christian God, the God Who Is, the Wholly Other who unaccountably came among us and forgave us for what we had made of ourselves.

Man cannot make God in his own image, even the finest image he knows. Yet this the social gospel did. It opened the way to worship of the God of collective bargaining, the God of desegregation, the God of minimum wage laws. These things may be fine or evil, but they are man-made, not given of God. It is one thing to search the Scripture, to ponder God's promises to man, to listen to the Holy Spirit, and to come to the conviction that this or that human remedy, imperfect and bungling though it may be, is more nearly true to his will than is its opposite or its absence. It is quite another thing, and indeed a deadly heresy, to use God as an authority for what one would like to see done. We are commanded to listen to him, to judge our actions by the touchstone of his will, not to enlist him as a sponsor for our fallible human endeavors.

The social gospel is insufficient. Its God is too small

and its concept of the Kingdom far too limited. It imagines that it can do God's job for him and build his Kingdom here on earth. This is one of man's vainest illusions. All that man can do, and that only with God's help, is to prepare for the Kingdom, to trust in it, to be attuned to its essential values, to know it when and as it comes. But at least the response of the social gospel is nearer to the Christian message and a more adequate answer than the acceptance of society as it is as God's providence itself. This attitude, which constitutes our fifth answer, was more prevalent in the eighteenth and nineteenth centuries than it is today. The lesson of the great depression has shaken our faith both in the divine origin and in the justice of our economic system, but as that lesson fades into history there are still some who may believe, with a witness who testified before the Royal Commission on the Aged Poor in London in 1895, that any form of old-age assistance is contrary to God's providence enshrined in the laws of supply and demand.

The social gospel is also more adequate than the sixth and seventh answers, which are the ones most often given by the church today.

The sixth, and perhaps the least important, is what might be called the church's institutional witness, the concern that the interests of religion be emphasized in a welfare program—that children in foster homes be encouraged to go to Sunday school or live with foster parents who will respect and nurture their faith, and the desire to tie assistance to instruction—to give, that is, a tract with the check. Some of this is undoubtedly good. Foster children, like all children, probably should be encouraged to go to Sunday school. But this seems, in all conscience, a very little concern to be the whole of the church's witness, and all too frequently it is tinged with the assumption that those being cared for by welfare programs need more instruction than those who are not. This borders not only on presumption but on the heresy that equates worldly success with grace—one of the great heresies of the church in its relation to welfare which will be explored in Chapter II.

The institutional answer is also a temptation to persons who see the church's witness as lying mainly in the moral sphere. This, the seventh inadequate answer, is admittedly a difficult matter. The church has a natural interest in reducing temptation and not encouraging sin or sins. If it genuinely believes that a welfare program is encouraging lust, or sloth, or possibly avarice—that is, immorality, dependence, or chiseling on relief—it has a duty to say so. But before it does so, it must be sure of at least two important things.

First, it must be sure of the facts. An excellent example is the often-expressed fear that Aid to Dependent Children, which makes grants to the mothers of illegitimate children because the children have no fathers, encourages immorality. It may seem on the surface that this is a fair judgment, but the evidence is against it. For many years after the establishment of the program the rate of illegitimate births did not rise at all. When it began to do so, within the last two or three years, the most probable causes lay in quite other things. A generation of young people in their most formative years were coming to adulthood in homes deprived of fathers because of World War II. Greater mobility and greater opportunity for men in places far from home strengthened a trend in those parts of our culture where most illegitimate births occur, making the woman the stable one of the family and giving the man a transitory role. Changing values in the whole of society had their influence. This does not excuse illegitimate births. They are a serious problem and one with which the church is properly concerned. But to blame public assistance for their occurrence is to make a naïve and a hasty judgment; nor is there any evidence that "stricter" welfare provisions, where these have been instituted—often to the real distress of numbers of innocent children—have managed to affect the problem.

And if this kind of judgment is fallible, how much more difficult it is to make a moral judgment in an individual case! People are in need for a multiplicity of reasons. Some are sick in an obvious way, or old, or deprived of parental support. Some have been made poor by the conditions of our fallen society. Their jobs are gone or their training is insufficient for the times. Some are sick in mind, confused, hopeless, or discouraged. In some, mind and body act together, as in psychosomatic conditions, which even medical science is only beginning to understand. These people may have no obvious disability, but are nonetheless disabled and cannot be cured by exhortation or by cutting them off relief. Some, it is true, are lazy or dishonest in other ways. A large segment is probably both a little sick and a little sinful and it would take the judgment of Solomon to tell how much of each. Sometimes welfare regulations have to be made broad enough so as not to punish those who are sick as though they were sinful, and thus include a few sinful too. Yet many church members presume to hand out moral judgments which those who know the people best find it impossible to make.

The second requirement before the church can properly make a moral judgment on a welfare program is that it remove the beam in its own eye before becoming moralistic about the mote in the eye of the welfare recipient. Apart from man's collective sin for the existence of much poverty there is the question of the temptations that extreme poverty involves. How hard would it be, for instance, to be entirely honest if a little dishonesty made the difference between deprivation for one's children and half-decent conditions? In many states today a welfare grant means three quarters of what home economists,

trained in the kind of careful management that few poor
people could achieve, hold is needed to live in minimum
health and decency. How many of us would find it hard
to be honest on an income of a dollar a day for rent,
clothing, food, and all other expenses? Yet some states allow no more for a single person. How many would not
be tempted when children's welfare is at stake? And how
many of the people who pass moral judgment on the
welfare recipient who cheats do not themselves, with far
less temptation to overcome, chisel on their income tax
and their expense accounts?

There is also the matter of a difference in sins. In our
fallen society some of the seven deadly sins receive much
more reprobation than others. The sin of sloth, for instance, the unwillingness to work, even though it is a
deadly sin when it is willful and not the result of sickness
in body or mind, is much more harshly punished by our
present economy than is avarice, gluttony, envy, or pride.
Indeed gluttony, which in modern terms might be called
conspicuous and unnecessary consumption, is at the moment highly favored and even praised on every hand. It
might be thought that the church, which knows that both
sloth and gluttony are sinful in God's sight, would be
tempted to redress the balance and show more mercy to
the sinner most highly disadvantaged by the world as it is.
But the difficulty lies in the fact that the leaders of the
church are more inclined themselves to gluttony than they
are to sloth. It is easy to condemn sins that one does not
have oneself.

In any case, however, the witness of the church to
morals and its claim to judge others by them, is an inadequate witness. The church is more than an arbiter of
morals. It is a body seeking to witness to an overwhelming
truth. And so often it has permitted this truth to escape
it or has failed to recognize its relevance to the world.

Modern welfare was in fact born of the church's failure

and of the failure of the small community which acted almost as if it was a local church with all of the church's exclusiveness and parochialism. It was born in reaction against the petty moralisms of the church, against the church's presumption in making hasty judgments of its fellows, against its tendency to care for its own and let the rest of the world go by, against its frequent lack of understanding of the causes of much poverty and unwillingness to accept its own guilt in creating much of it, against its all-too-frequent lack of mercy, and against its tendency to rely on the self-satisfying emotion of a patronizing pity rather than on the stern call of an adequate Christian stewardship.

Is it surprising then that welfare has grown away from the church, that it has looked to other philosophies or formed its own professional creeds? If the church is to regain its rightful leadership in the field, it must face the challenge of these secular philosophies.

This is the challenge really to witness to what the gospel means. It is to regain a Christian perspective, to relate what is happening today to its ultimate convictions, to show once again that the amazing gospel of our Lord Jesus Christ has relevance to the problem of human need. It is to act as stimulator of what should be done: as example in what it does itself, and as critic where it finds that it has a relevant insight.

This is not an easy task. It requires both care and prayer. It demands both an examination of what the Christian message is and an understanding of what its contribution can be. The church, for instance, must never forget that it does not have detailed competence in the welfare field. Modern welfare is by necessity a very complex matter, involving considerations of economics, social conditions, public order, political necessity, psychology, and a knowledge of the helping process. In these the church's judgments may be, and often are, both naïve and impulsive. The church's witness must be, in fact, to goals, to principles, to concepts about the nature of man and his purpose upon which programs may be built or trends checked and reconsidered. The church, for instance, cannot say that recipients of old-age assistance should or should not be allowed to own a radio or a TV. That is a wholly professional judgment. It depends on such things as available funds and other resources in the community. But it might, if it were convinced of the principle, witness to whether society should require that the aged poor forgo all forms of recreation. It might ponder whether a man's dignity is increased by giving him little to live for. The church might raise the question of whether a man's needs as a human being are more or less important than making an example of him because he has been unable to save. It might have something to say about the kind of conditions that we impose on those who ask our aid and of our purpose in helping them.

It is this kind of question, far-reaching in its implications, that the church has for the most part ignored or answered in generalities so broad that they have ceased to be specifically Christian. And it is to these questions that the church, with its radical doctrine of who man is and what is ultimately demanded of him, could perhaps come up with answers that reflect, at least in part, God's will.

This book is a search for some of these answers, based on a conviction that the gospel the church proclaims is more than relevant—that it is, in fact, the only ultimate solution—and on a knowledge of welfare and those who live by it. The search may uncover some startling answers that will offend some of our preconceptions, but the Christian gospel has always been disturbing and startling news.

Chapter II

The Three Great Heresies of
the Church Regarding Welfare

IT IS ALWAYS EASIER TO LOOK AT HERESIES IF WE
think of them as historical facts. The Arians, the Ar-
minians, the Docetists, or the Manichees—we know or
can find out quite easily what they believed and how they
distorted the gospel. It is harder to see heresy in ourselves. But sometimes if we look at the mistakes of others
we can see our own. This is my reason for dipping now
into the past—that we may see ourselves in it.

Heresies also occur when there is a difficult question
to answer. And in the matter of the poor there are at least
two difficult questions, closely interrelated, that every
age has sought to answer in a somewhat different way.

The first is the cause of poverty. Is it God's action or
man's? Has God ordained poverty, either individually—
for the good or for the punishment of the individual—
or for some wider purpose? Or is poverty the result of
man's fallen state, either individually or collectively? The
second question is how, and to what extent, the giver is
responsible for the use made of the gift. To what extent
should the provision of relief to the poor be an act of pure
love, a treating one's neighbor as oneself, and to what
extent should it be an attempt to reform him? To what
extent is giving harmful to the character of the recipient?
How much should his use of the gift be controlled?

18

These are still the central questions in the welfare field today. And still we are confused by them. Some of us think that we have the answer, but all too often we are, in fact, confused by one of the heresies into which our church or our culture has fallen along the way.

The very early Christians had no doubt at all. They felt an outpouring of love, which took the form of holding all things in common. But as the Christian community grew and became identified with society instead of remaining a little group within it, problems began to arise. Some of them are obvious even in the epistles. The major problem was the question of how one could judge rightly in giving relief. This we will take up later. But a very serious problem began to arise in the relationship between the giver and the recipient, and there are many traces of this heresy today.

The ancient church, and indeed the church as late as the nineteenth century, believed more strongly than we do in God's providence in social affairs. As a stanza, generally omitted today, of the hymn "All Things Bright and Beautiful" has it, "The rich man in his castle, the poor man at his gate; God put them in their places and ordered their estate." For a time the church played with the theory that poverty was somehow holy. Because some saints chose poverty as a way of ridding themselves of worldly preoccupation the church was apt to hold that poverty was ordained by God for the poor person's salvation. There are still some pious souls who have never been poor or deprived who are not free of this concept. An orphan deprived of family life is thought somehow to be "lucky" because of the difficulties he has had to overcome. But the concept soon proved unworkable, if only because men were forced to recognize that many of the poor were far from holy or blessed.

Men therefore turned to the theory that the poor must be, in Chrysostom's term, designed by God to be "useful" to the rich in giving them a chance to get rid of their abundance and win treasure in heaven. Charity soon became the one certain way to salvation, perhaps to some extent because the former way, martyrdom, was no longer available. Cyprian describes charity as "needful for the weak"—for which he might be commended—but also as "glorious for the strong, assisted by which the Christian accomplishes spiritual grace, deserves well of Christ the judge, accounts God his debtor."

This was the great heresy of the medieval church. It divorced charity and stewardship from any real love or justice. It did not die with the Reformation. An Anglican in the eighteenth century put it neatly: charity is a loan to God which he engages himself to repay.

Such bargaining with the Almighty may seem distasteful, but is it so very foreign from some of our practices today? What about the benefactor who patronizes the "poor little orphans" in a church home? Is his or her impulse really one of Christian love, or does the giving accrue more to the giver than to the recipient? What about the emotion of pity, which often means a sense of superiority? What about the all-too-frequent demand that the recipient be grateful or show due respect? How different is this concept of the poor man's responsibility from the role assigned to him in the apocryphal gospel *The Shepherd of Hermas*, which is to pray for the rich? How much demand for personal, voluntary giving, and how much dissatisfaction with professionalism in modern welfare is not due to the feeling that giving should receive its reward?

But this heresy, great as it was, and persistent as it still is, was as nothing to that which arose over the question of the judgment that man should use in distributing alms. The problem arose early. As early as the second century we find discussions of "prudence" in almsgiving. Evidently men and churches were making hasty judgments. Basil says that it takes great experience to distinguish between those who are really poor and those who beg only in order to collect money; other Fathers held that gifts to the undeserving were a lesser evil than overlooking the deserving—a point of view that could well be stressed today.

It was left to Chrysostom to put forward a wholly Christian point of view. His answer was that a personal judgment was impossible, both pragmatically and theologically. How could man, who was such a sinner, and who had been given so much that he did not deserve by God, judge another man's desert? To do so was not so much to prove the recipient unworthy of the giver's liberality as to prove the giver unworthy of God's. This understanding brought Chrysostom to positions that are startlingly like modern humanistic thought, but from a theological base. "The poor," he says, "have only one recommendation: their need. If he be the most perverse of all men, should he lack necessary food we ought to appease his hunger." He had a deep understanding of the temptations of the poor. Even, he says, if a man is practicing imposture, he is to be pitied in that he needed to do it. He would also have the citizens of Alexandria not confine their relief to their fellow townsmen because even to give relief to someone attracted to the city by its generosity was a tribute to it—a very different point of view from that of states which today maintain strict residence requirements for those to whom they will offer aid.

Chrysostom was no cloistered monk. He was Bishop of Alexandria, and dispensed its relief. He had recognized an essential Christian truth, but it could well be objected that his principles needed modification to be practical in this fallen world. This was very nearly done by Thomas Aquinas, who in his magnificent attempt to reconcile heaven and earth saw clearly that the only solution to the judgmentalism of man was the judgment of the law, which he considered to be a reflection, however imperfect, of God's will. Thomas, and Ambrose before him, insist that benevolence has to do with justice and not with charity. It may be that this was too radical a conclusion, threatening the picture of order that he was striving to create, for Thomas placed this justice in the realm of moral law and not as the subject of enforceable statute. It was left to the framers of the Social Security Acts of the world in the twentieth century to arrive by a different pathway at the concept of a legal right to subsistence under certain conditions of need. This is nominally the law in America today.

Thus there are sound theological reasons for the eschewing of personal judgment and the establishment in law of a "right to assistance" under certain conditions, and indeed medieval society at times approached this ideal. In Ypres and Bruges in the sixteenth century Juan de Vives established a system of collective responsibility for the needs of the poor that was remarkable for its justice and for its absence of condescension toward those in need. The Religious College of France called it "hard" but "according to the Scriptures"—"hard," one might presume, because it eliminated giving for the givers' sake.

The Reformation is sometimes blamed for sweeping all this away. But the fault lay not in the Reformation, not in the essential doctrines of Calvin and Luther, but in the use that was made of them to conform to the world. Calvin's belief in the unmerited love of God was just as strong as Chrysostom's and his sense of duty was not far from Thomas' sense of justice. The early writings of John Knox are full of compassion for the poor, whom, he says, God the Father, Jesus Christ, and the Holy Spirit speaking by Paul "have so earnestly commended to oure cayre," and whom he accuses the papists of having neglected.

Nevertheless, before long, and as certain doctrines were either emphasized or modified as in Puritan New England, the poor were reduced to an inferior class both socially and morally. In private charity personal judgments were allowed to flourish and might sometimes be favorable, but in the public sphere—and state programs were beginning to be established because of the fragmentation of the church—the judgment was universally negative. So far from establishing any sort of "right to subsistence," the law was used mainly to punish those on relief. There were a few attempts to classify, in rough and ready terms, such as the Elizabethan Bishop Ridley's "poore by impotencie, poore by casualtie, and the thriftles poore," but theology itself was quick to break this down. The poor became identified with those who were not elect. Human success and God's favor gradually became identified.

There have been many explanations of how this came about. Economic liberalism and an enhanced sense of the inviolability of personal property; a new emphasis on work as a primary Christian virtue, due perhaps to Luther's insistence on vocation or to the increasing demands of an industrial society; the uncertainty of "the saints" as to their own election, and therefore their search for outward signs, have all been given as reasons. So has the theory that the "saints" knew sin and thought that they could cure it, whereas they admitted themselves helpless in the face of psychology or more complex economic trends. But the underlying answer is the same. Man was not really prepared to believe what the gospel taught him: that all men are genuinely sinners, that before God there is so little difference between the best and the worst of them, that God commands us not to judge but to respect and forgive our fellows, and that even in this imperfect world the purpose of law should be to enhance and not to restrict the right to life. Man could not believe that his worldly activities did not earn him "merit" in the sense of the right to judge and to control those who had not the same fortune. To him "original sin" was something that belonged to the other fellow, and "grace" was the perquisite of himself and those like him.

God, in fact, became identified with the interests of the successful, with the institution of private property, and with the civic virtues. He was no longer the Wholly Other, the Unknowable, before whom even the best of men merited damnation. And the poor—they were actually called so once—were thought of as an insult to him.

The result was that misfortune became almost as much of a sin as laziness or vice. The poor, good or bad, lazy or unfortunate, "deserving" or "undeserving," were treated as a class little, if any, better than criminals. Any kind of mercy or forgiveness for them was ruled out. As an English "expert" on the poor law, a churchman, said less than seventy years ago, "Kindness to an individual too often means cruelty to a class." The remedy was clearly to make the life of the poor person just as bleak, as gloomy, and as unpleasant as it was possible to do.

This meant in practice the workhouse test—the forcing of the poor out of their homes and into public institutions on the theory that only those who were really indigent would accept such degradation. It meant the loss of civil rights. As late as 1889 a farmer in Kansas lost the custody of his children solely on the grounds that he had accepted public relief as a result of a crippling drought. And it meant that the poor were deliberately allowed less to live on than the poorest laborer could possibly earn, so that the poor person might be spurred to greater efforts. Any possibility that it is love and not repression which overcomes evil—a lesson man might have learned from the cross—was forgotten in this relationship. For two or three hundred years the only man who seems to have understood that to be merciful to a sinner may not be to encourage vice but to give him new courage and who pleaded for a little joy in the lives of the destitute was that old reprobate and penitent sinner, Dr. Samuel Johnson. The fact that his concept of "a little joy" included a few pennies to spend on gin should not blind us to his essential understanding.

Along with this repression went the demand on the poor for a higher standard of morality than was required of the self-sufficient. The pauper was not only required to be thankful and humble; he was "preached at" at every turn. Any deviation from the path of the strictest morality cost him his means of livelihood and he was expected to surrender all control of his normal business to the judgment of his superiors. He could be forbidden to marry, or if he were married, his children became, as it were, public property. How anyone ever expected him to regain his self-respect or to have the strength to assert his independence is indeed hard to see.

The picture in fact looks most unchristian. But doesn't much of this heresy still exist today? Don't many of us instinctively judge all public-assistance recipients by the few who seem to us unwilling to work? Don't many of us argue for more "control" of relief expenditures, for better "supervision" of the lives of those in need? Don't many of us demand a higher standard of morality among those on relief than we do of our fellows? How many of us are concerned that a man who asks for help retain his dignity in this crisis? How many of us deny to those on relief a minimum health and decency standard?

Let us look at several examples. The past few years have seen a resurgence, until the Federal Government intervened, of what are known as "suitable home" provisions in the program of Aid to Dependent Children. These laws in fact permit the state to force a child to starve or to be removed from his parents, not because the parents have been found guilty of neglect or the child is in need of protection by due process of law, but because the welfare department has made a judgment that the home does not meet its standards. The action is taken by withdrawing the grant. Is this not one law for those who have to ask for relief and another for those who do not? The most general grounds for this decision is a moral one. But how many "better class" homes are not equally immoral, and no one takes any action?

Again, let us look at the newspapers. How many articles does one see that deal sympathetically, with tolerance and understanding, with the plight of the family on relief, the struggle, even the shame? The great majority emphasize the few who cheat or misbehave. Even the "comics" co-operate. Jokes too often subtly suggest that all who receive relief are dishonest. A filler in today's paper reads: "Nowadays everyone needs a car, if only to collect one's check from the welfare department." Does this humorist know how many families in isolated rural districts have had to give up their only contact with the outside world to be granted enough to eat?

How many people think about need, and how many more only about deterrence? How many have any idea what a public assistance grant will buy? How many know that their state grants less than a minimum health and decency budget and then expects recipients to be both healthy and decent? How many are much more concerned that relief may be "attractive" to people than disturbed at economic conditions that make it possible for such a miserable existence to be attractive to anyone? When a relief client buys some candy for his children, how many well-to-do people consider what it means never to have the slightest chance to give one's children anything not entirely utilitarian, and don't many blame him for poor management or deceit?

The same goes for our private giving. At Christmas many welfare agencies, public and private, ask for funds for Christmas dinners or presents for children. Most people respond, but with moral strings attached. Presents are to be given only to the children of "good" parents who will show appreciation. A "good" church family complained to our welfare department recently that their dinner went to children whose father was in jail. Who needs friendship most, the child whose father is in jail or the child whose father is at home? Whom did Christ come to save—the sinners or the good?

Indeed, the moralistic heresy is alive today. The church becomes too easily the guardian of our cultural heritage. It rubs in the lessons that society teaches. It contributes nothing different, no new understanding of man.

There will be people who will protest that the church has often, in its history, been the conscience of the people with regard to social injustice. This certainly seemed to be so at the time of the Evangelical Revival. In Great Britain, where it began, this was the time of the great humanitarian measures, the Reform Bill and the Factory Acts. It was also the beginning of the age of great philanthropies, of the founding of schools and colleges, orphanages, and other charities.

The reform movement was primarily religious. Two elements seem to have been important. One was the growing understanding that all men, being loved of God, had a worth that could not be denied. The other was the recognition that the rich were also sinful. Indeed much of the philanthropy was a kind of "fire insurance," a penitence for greed and for preoccupation with material gain. Wesley himself was much aware of this dilemma. He believed that religion would help a man prosper, that industry and frugality would inevitably bring riches, but he was also aware that possessions were a snare. His proffered solution was that a man should gain all that he could, save all that he could, but also give all that he could, and therefore "grow in grace" and "lay up treasure in heaven."

Yet the same Parliament that passed the Reform Bill of

1832 passed the Poor Law of 1834 that established work-houses and forced paupers to choose between starvation and the workhouse's deliberately contrived gloom, discomfort, and lack of hope. It was as if society was willing to consider the rights of those who contributed to the rich man's treasure, but denied them to people who were unproductive. Even the Evangelical churches were servants of our economy.

Some have explained this by noting that the Evangelicals cared more about personal, individual sins than they did about sin. Wesley, says Richard Niebuhr in his *Social Sources of Denominationalism,* "was more offended by blasphemous use of the name of God than by a blasphemous use of his creatures."

But there was a deeper reason. There is another heresy here, perhaps not so obvious but nevertheless a very real one. If we call giving for the sake of the giver's soul the great Catholic heresy, and moralism in relief the corresponding Protestant one, this might be called the modernist heresy. Its primary characteristic is paternalism, and theologically it arises from lack of understanding of what is meant by original sin.

In welfare we have seen how Puritan thinking tended to pervert this doctrine into sin for the other fellow and grace for me and mine. The natural religious reaction to this trend was to stress man's natural goodness, the presence of God in every man. This emphasis was badly needed, as it sometimes is today. But to reject in its name recognition of man's shared sinfulness, of his common predicament, of the actual fallen state of the world, is to lose an important source of understanding.

The great humanitarian movement of the nineteenth century was more or less based on this denial. It came in part, it is true, from the Methodists with their emphasis on God's indwelling grace, but also and much more strongly from the Quakers and the Unitarians, of whom a historian of welfare writes that they were not "hampered by belief in original sin."

This relieved the poor from the stricture of belonging to a sinful class and indeed provided a bridge between rich and poor that had not existed for several centuries. But because it in general approved the world as the better sort of people conceived it, Christian liberalism failed to see man's common responsibility for the conditions that breed poverty. It believed that what the poor man needed was not so much the means to live his own life, but the example and the guidance of the educated and the successful. And this in practice meant three principles that still color the church's concept of what welfare ought to be. For paternalism is a very active heresy and is so much a part of the thinking of many people that it does not look. like a heresy at all.

The three principles are "the personal touch," "guidance," and an ignoring of man's material needs in favor of counseling, exhortation, or as social workers sometimes express the same concepts today, "services" or "treatment." This is not to say that services, or even "treatment," may not often be needed. It is to say that they do not meet all the needs of a man. Men are not poor only because they lack education, guidance, or an ability to adjust to life. Man has an obligation, in simple justice or in atonement, to provide for others who have been denied the means to live a decent life. Jesus said, "Man does not live by bread alone," but he never denied the need for bread. In fact, he enjoined us to pray for it.

The finest expression of this kind of welfare was what became known as "friendly visiting" and sometimes as "Christian socialism" (which has nothing to do with Karl Marx). It sought to elevate the poor, but at its best also had ideals of friendship. Thomas Chalmers, a Scots Presbyterian minister who was one of its earliest exponents, was opposed to the workhouse as he saw it in England:

"Their paupers are met by the same treatment as their criminals." He also had the grace to write, somewhat cautiously, that "by putting ourselves under the roof of a poor neighbour, we in a manner render him for the time our superior," an enormous concession for the early nineteenth century. It still would be so for many people today.

But love between equals cannot exist with a sense of superiority or a desire to reform. Chalmers, and all like him, are much too apt to fall into giving, not what a person needs, but what the giver thinks he ought to have. And generally this meant few comforts, a balanced diet, and a kindly mentor or father figure. There is something pharisaical about the follower of Chalmers of whom it was said that the poor "soon came to understand the man who was as liberal with his sympathy as he was chary with meat and coal tickets," and who said himself, "I am beginning seriously to believe that all bodily aid to the poor is a mistake."

Ambrose had said, several centuries earlier, that to give "without good will," without the interests of the recipient at heart, is harmful both to the giver and to the man who receives. The nineteenth century, however, turned Chalmers' paternalism into organized charity and parceled it out, in a cautious manner, in accordance with what its dispensers believed to be the "good" of the poor. Although their judgment was largely moral, they began to call to their aid the infant social sciences, and in doing so began the transition to another attempt to answer the church's and society's problem about how to give wisely.

For let us be clear, objection to Chalmers' paternalism or to the Puritan's reprobation of the poor does not call on man to abdicate judgment. Christianity demands justice and love, not indulgence. If it should not be concerned with punishing him for his sins, nor arranging his life for him, neither is it called on to maintain the unfortunate in luxury or to remove normal responsibility from him. The problem is not to eliminate judgment, but to discover, in this fallen world, the way to make it most nearly in accord with a Christian view of man's relationship to his fellows.

There are three possible sources of judgment which the church might consider. The first of these is the "judgment of the saint," or, in welfare, giving to people what the "best" people think they deserve. This is what the Puritans used and what Chalmers made more kindly, but still employed as his guiding principle. It is what many church people still want to use today. And this, despite its apparent connection with religious principle, is the least Christian of the three and was what Jesus meant, surely, when he told us not to judge lest we be judged ourselves. It is the assumption that we know enough about other people to pass moral judgment on them. This is seeing the mote in our neighbor's eye and ignoring the beam in our own. It is pre-empting God's judgment and eating of the tree of the knowledge of good and evil, contrary to his command.

The second might be called the "judgment of the scientist," or giving to people what it is thought they need. This allows a little less scope for the giver's predilections. It is the form of judgment most favored by today's society, and the one that the later nineteenth century began to call to its aid, but it too can lead to pride and to the assumption that judgment is a "right" exercised by those who know over those who do not. But judgment is not a "right." It is a regrettable necessity, to be exercised with a due sense of humility. When it becomes more than this, it is unchristian.

The third is judgment by the law, or the giving to people that to which society holds they are entitled. Although law may be thought of as secular, and is often illogical and harsh, there is much to recommend it from the Christian point of view. It does not pretend to be anything but human. It knows itself to be an adjustment to an imperfect world. It is the least personal, and therefore in a way the most humble of all methods of judgment. The judge who tries to impose his personal will on others is restrained by the collective wisdom or foolishness of the last thousand years. And specifically it is rooted in the belief in equal rights, in the denial that wealth or position or superior knowledge or morality give to anyone the right to judge or to control his fellows. That it is sometimes abused in practice does not invalidate its attempt to arrive at common and humble judgment.

Thomas said the human law is a reflection of the divine, however imperfect or perverted. If this is so, the role of the church might be thought of as in part, at least, to illumine the law with its Christian insights and not to substitute for it its own more personal judgments. In the welfare field this means striving to help men create a law, a policy, or a procedure that is fair, generous, prudent, and that preserves the dignity of even the most disadvantaged.

Chapter III

The Humanist Challenge

THIS AGE HAS SEEN THE GREATEST ADVANCE IN THE practical expression of man's love for his fellow in distress, and is already in danger of losing what it has won. For the contribution that humanism brought to the problem is like the seed that fell in shallow earth and flourished mightily, but could not maintain its growth, or rather, will not be able to do so unless it is transplanted or fertilized, or somehow given firmer roots. But the plant showed real promise and put the church's weeds to shame.

What really started the germination and made this age the most exciting and potentially the most Christian in its understanding of the problems of the poor and the troubled were two happenings, neither even remotely religious.

The first was the great depression. Quite suddenly millions of people, who could not be considered by any scale of human judgment improvident, lazy, or lacking in moral fiber, fell into need and had to ask for help. Those who had any concept of sin were forced to reconsider their bland assumption that it was the individual who was always the sinner and society that was always good. Indeed this process had been going on for some time. As early as 1909, in an earlier depression, Mrs. Sidney Webb, in England, had spoken of a "new consciousness" of sin that lay not in the individual but in the kind of society that deprived so many of so much in life. But it was the great depression that convinced America of universal sin.

The second was analytical psychology, or in other words, Sigmund Freud.

This may be hard to swallow for those who see in Freud only a mandate for sexual license (which Freud himself never taught) or a kind of determinism that would seem to rob a man of any responsibility for his actions. How could Freud, who thought religion to be an illusion, conduce to a more nearly Christian handling of man's welfare problems?

He made two very great contributions. The first was that the new psychology was at first a great corrective to pride. Freud's major message was that mental distress, and indeed character disorder, was not something that some people have and from which others are entirely free. It was rather an exaggeration of trends that all human beings share. Health and sickness, like sin and virtue, were not opposites but passed insensibly into each other. The world was not all black or white, good and bad, sick and well, but a whole succession of grays. And therefore all men were vulnerable and all capable of recovery, and no man could afford to cast the first stone at his neighbor. His "discovery" of the unconscious, of the irrational forces that shape even our most logical and abstract thinking, only echoes Paul's dilemma: "For I do not do the good I want, but the evil I do not want is what I do" (Rom. 7:19). Man cannot become good through a simple act of will.

The second is that in his method, in his listening to people, in his attempt to understand the meaning to them of events in their lives, he made possible an exercise of a Christian virtue that had too long been neglected. This was empathy, the effort to see the world through another man's eyes and know what it means to him. Empathy, the ability to feel *with* people, is as superior to sympathy, or feeling *like* them as sympathy is to pity, which is feeling *about* them. It is in a very small way the feeling God must have for man, which treats as important what man wants and how he feels. It is treating man as the subject of the sentence, the person whose actions determine the outcome, and not as the object, the thing done to, or studied or felt about.

To the new concept of welfare analytical psychology contributed, then, empathy and a sense of "there, but for the grace of God, go I." The depression heightened man's understanding both of his own vulnerability and of the fact that the world was indeed fallen if it could be so indiscriminately cruel and unfair. It helped man turn to law and justice as the source of his welfare judgments. The law had been used formerly only to repress those in need (as late as 1940, fifteen states denied paupers the right to vote). Now it was used to establish a right on the part of those who had suffered calamity to assistance from society. In part this was done by compulsory insurance. In part, where it was clear that there was no possibility of premiums being paid because of the lifelong poverty of a group, legal "eligibility" was established to what was sometimes called an "uncovenanted insurance." This was done for those who were old or blind, or, as children, deprived of the care and support of a parent. The Government specifically required that these people be treated with dignity. No one was to tell them how to spend the money that was provided for them. No one was to treat them as inferior human beings, to hold them up to public shame, or to demand of them behavior that was not demanded of the populace as a whole. Yet the payment was not to be a dole to anyone who preferred relief to work. A man must be genuinely sick or unavailable before his children could be helped; there was to be careful determination of objective need. It was understood that there would be a few who would try to cheat, just as there are in any human undertaking, but this would not invalidate the basic principle, any more than occasional vote frauds invalidate our belief in the essential rightness of the ballot box.

At the same time there began to take shape a new profession, one of several new helping professions, devoted to trying to understand the individual problems of people, to extend empathy to them, to help them fulfill themselves as human beings. This profession, social work, emphasized both learning and self-discipline in the training of its practitioners. It strove to help through relationship —a relationship of love, as one writer put it, "completely oriented to the individual's needs and serving his purposes only." It might have taken as its charter I Cor., ch. 13. But it listened to Freud and not to the church. Why? Because the church was so committed to making moral judgments about people and relying on exhortation and punishment to gain its ends. Because the church clung to its "right" to give personally, out of impulse and not out of a real feeling for the recipient. Because the church denied that there was anything to learn about the needs of other people or how they could be helped and insisted that good intentions were enough. And, of course, because the church was afraid when the new professions listened to the new, strange doctrine. Instead of trying to find out what truth there might be in it, the church virtually excommunicated those who were tainted by it. Is it surprising that as a result many social workers themselves turned against the church and that the gap between religion and social work widened?

Part of the problem lay in the fact that the church and its allies had proved insufficient to the day. Not only church charity but local relief and even the great voluntary agencies were unequal to the task. Voluntarism became an issue. The Red Cross refused to accept twenty-five million dollars that President Hoover wished to make available to it. On the part of the church, fears of blurring the distinction between church and state became, as they often do, symbols of opposition and distrust rather than of co-operation. The state was left to carry the overwhelming welfare load.

The church could have recognized that its leadership would still be needed. But instead it felt aggrieved. It did not seem to see that it was being chastened, that it had too often lost the power of love, and that the wave of humanism which swept over the country was a necessary corrective to its attitude of superiority and to its desire to get satisfaction through its giving.

The church did not repent. If it had done so, it might have retained its leadership in the field. It not only might have illumined some of the truths to which the humanists were struggling but it might have helped them see more clearly or earlier some of their mistakes. It could have strengthened their new-found understanding that one man cannot judge another except where he must, by human law, make a fallible decision in the interest of social order. How could it have forgotten what, to paraphrase John Knox, not only Jesus Christ himself but the Holy Spirit speaking through Paul had so explicitly commanded? The church could also have helped the humanists see that freedom does not consist in unlimited choice about non-essentials but in responsible choice about essentials. Thereby the field might have been saved from a good deal of silly theory and perhaps even sillier practice that confused freedom with indulgence or permissiveness. The church could have helped the new profession understand better what is meant by responsibility and how this can be helpful if it is not insisted upon punitively.

The church could, in fact, have saved humanism from one of its prevalent errors, sentimentality. It could have tempered the psychologist's and the social worker's in-

sistence on pain and loss as the major human ills by pointing out that although we are commanded to relieve suffering where we can, man may still choose suffering as the
means to something higher, or accept it as the price of
his endeavor. Did not our Lord himself do so? And it is
still better to have loved and lost than never to have loved
at all, although much of modern psychology would seem
to say, "Do not love, or you might be hurt."

The church could have testified to many things that it
knew, if it had once stopped to think about it. It knows
much about helping, for it has before it the example of
divine helping. It knows how hard it is to accept help and
how stubbornly man demands help on his own terms. It
knows that if man is too anxious about worldy affairs he
has little room in his life for God. Who knows better than
the church that true love permits to its object freedom
to choose? Can it forget the very first of its sacred books?
It has a magnificent testimony to make about the worth
of each individual and about the possibility of his redemption, even though it may differ from the humanist
in its insistence that God must have a part to play in it.
And above all, it could have helped the humanists to
remain humble, making clear that man is not a mechani-
cal being whose workings can be ultimately known and
manipulated. He is something more than that.

But the church did none of these things. This was a
double tragedy. In the first place the church has been
among the forces that have made the most humane, hopeful, and "Christian" welfare system that America has
known less successful than it ought to be.

Much has been written and said lately about the "failure" of this system. It has been accused of fostering dependence. Cases have been cited of families who have
been on relief for three generations. Even the Secretary
of Health, Education, and Welfare has said that we have
been working on the wrong philosophy. But the "wrong

philosophy" has not been that of the right to assistance.
It has been our failure, to which the church has contributed, really to implement this right.

Judged by standards that really matter, by the health
and vigor, the hopefulness in the lives of those who are
in need, their freedom of choice, their ability to exercise
normal human rights and undertake normal responsibility,
our system has not been given the chance to show what
it can do. Its dignity has been slowly whittled away, by
making relief rolls less confidential, by "suitable home"
provisions, by demands that there be control of how a
family spends its money, and above all, by continuing
wholly insufficient grants, which are below the health
and decency level. A man cannot be self-respecting if we
take respect from him, nor responsible if we deny him
responsibility. He cannot be vigorous if we underfeed him,
nor secure enough to assert his independence if we keep
him insecure. Throughout the centuries we have tried to
force man into self-reliance by punishing him or treating
him like a child. It has not worked. It cannot work. Punishment does not touch the root of the problem, even with
the few who are inclined to dishonesty. It is not by shaming people or making their decisions for them that men
were, are, and will be redeemed. It is by an immense
valuation of even the poorest and sorriest of them. Our
system has been too Christian to be accepted. More has
also been expected of it than any system could deliver.
The system has been expected to cure all social ills—ille-
gitimacy, family breakdown, lack of education and skill.
It is blamed because there are still, in an economy of
plenty, many people who are in need. Yet the belief that
he can abolish poverty is one of man's fondest illusions.
God almost seems to take a delight in showing him that
he cannot do so. Every new "advance" in social conditions creates a new category of need, as improvements in
medicine have in our days created need among the aged

and replaced a few "orphans" with a greater number of children whose parents are alive but sick. Undoubtedly there are many families today who will be permanently in need and whose children may be the same, although it may surprise some people to know, for instance, that a greater proportion of the population of supposedly self-reliant colonial Virginia received public relief than do in the same state today.

There are, of course, improvements that should be made. More skilled help is needed for families at the point of breakdown and relief needs to be given in a less grudging or degrading way. More opportunities need to be offered for people to enhance their health or their vocational skills. But the answer is not to go back on the dignity of relief. It is to make it a more responsible, dignified thing.

The second tragedy is the church's failure to make its witness when the humanist professions themselves became infected with pride. For humanism is not the answer. Although the humanists exercised for a time a loving-kindness and a valuation of man that should have been the church's prerogative, humanism contains in it an element that negates its belief in the dignity of man. It is a strange paradox indeed, but when a movement starts with the premise that man is naturally "good," it ends by discovering man's weakness and the need of the strong to control the weak. If, on the other hand, it starts with man's sinful nature, including that of its own leaders, it finds the good, the God, in him. As F. R. Barry has said in his *Relevance of Christianity*, "This bouyant attitude which built its confidence on belief in man, certain that he needed God no longer, has ended in such a disbelief in man, such radical distrust in human nature, that the world is half paralyzed by reason of it."

The process is amply illustrated by the Russian revolution. Marx and Lenin believed that when the economic injustice of capitalism was abolished, man, being naturally good, would need no state to control him. The state would "wither away." No documentation is needed to see what has happened. When man creates his utopia, his kingdom of heaven on earth, he goes on being sinful or inadequate or maladjusted. But since he has now no excuse, it can only be that some men are wicked, or weak, or subject to evil influence from outside, and this finally comes to include everyone but the ruling clique, which then becomes the instrument of indoctrination or repression. At first this usually takes the form of a benevolent authority acting for the deviant's good or out of compassion for him. In the end it subjects him to his culture or to the state.

What has this to do with welfare, or with social work today? Precisely that the judgment of law, which the humanists supported while they retained some of science's humility and its determinism, is being replaced by the judgment of the scientist. Already the system of legal rights in the public assistance provisions of the Social Security Act has been weakened by the pronouncement, enacted in 1956, that its purpose is to rehabilitate people or to preserve family life. These sound like worthy goals and their danger may not be clear, but they have subtly changed the empasis from what a man is entitled to, to what society wants for him. It changes him from subject to object. It re-creates the categories of those who need to be "rehabilitated" or "changed" and those who will bring this change about—the sinner and the righteous, the maladjusted and the adjusters.

It makes no radical difference that this paternalism is intended to foster man's ability to exercise his inherent right to self-fulfillment, which is its professional rationale. Nor does it matter so much that the methods used to induce change rely more largely on influence, persuasion, and kindness than they do on commands and threats, for, as we have discovered in the world of advertising and through the techniques known as "brainwashing," indirect and apparently unthreatening means may often be harder to combat than direct commands. It does not alter the basic argument that this philosophy is growing among a group of people who have demonstrated their love and respect for people. It is exactly within the framework of good will and good intentions that sin begins. It was in its good intentions that the charity of the church became the most sinful.

The fact remains that one segment of the population is claiming the right to control the lives of another in the name of science, which is itself identified with our present culture.

A glance at current social work literature confirms this fact. While any quotations are necessarily out of context, it is in straws in the wind, in the gradual infestation of the good, that this kind of sin develops. Social workers are already claiming to be "authoritative," although they eschew authoritarianism. They are claiming the right to "exercise social control," to be "authoritative," to "intervene" in the lives of others wherever maladjustment is noted between the individual and his environment, even to be an "ego ideal" for the inadequate client and to represent to him "the core values of our culture." And the "ethic of responsibility," which these quotations from recent social-work publications exemplify, is justified by the possession of "knowledge and skills unknown to those who worked many years before us." Granted that a parent who is neglecting his children is difficult to understand, there are both pride and devaluation in a statement such as the following: "To the stunted, feeble personality that is the neglectful parent, the agency, through the worker, becomes a model on which to pattern his own growth."

The serious thing about this trend is the loss of a life-giving principle. It is not so much what has happened to people as what may happen that is important. The "new purpose" of public assistance has not resulted in much actual denial of rights. But it has introduced a new attitude. Public assistance is presented, not as the client's right, but as something given to him to rehabilitate him under social-work help and guidance. More guardians and conservators are being appointed to control the recipient's funds. More privacy is being invaded for the client's or society's good. There is a tendency to deprive more people of their right to control their own affairs more easily on the basis of a negative diagnosis or a finding of "ego deficiency."

All this may not sound very dreadful. But the tragedy is that humanism, which formerly challenged the church's moralism and its overidentification with the world as it is, is reinforcing this heresy and, in fact, going beyond it. No wonder there is talk of the reconciliation between the church and social work! While there is a genuine reconciliation between the gospel and certain social-work principles that can and should be made, all too often it is the wrong kind of social science and a heresy in the church that are becoming reconciled.

Again, how far do we intend to go with "social control"? Social control is the ultimate weapon of the totalitarian. Although at the moment this control is benevolent, it must not be forgotten that there are no inherent limits to the scientist's pride. But to the moralistic pride of the church there is always the limit of God's "Otherness," his ultimately unknowable will. Although the church may forget it temporarily, in the end the church must recognize humility as an essential virtue. The scientist has no such checks upon pride. This is particularly true when his "good" is the culture in which he lives. It is not for nothing that extrapolations like Huxley's *Brave New World* or Orwell's *1984* predict that the social sciences will serve those who rule the world, by "conditioning" the people to a complacent subservience. So far the church has done little to witness to the dangers that it knows inevitably attend such pride.

What checks there have been have come from the legal profession. This profession, for instance, while not denying the importance of individualized justice in the juvenile courts, has helped these courts become more aware of the rights of young people brought before them. Lawyers have done much to formulate and maintain the "rights" nature of public assistance. It was Delafield Smith, an attorney, who said at the 1946 National Conference of Social Work: "The independence and unplanned, unregimented freedom of action of its rich and powerful members is not the test of a free society. . . . [This is] to be found in the scope and privilege reserved to, and possessed by, its weakest elements, those who are under the greatest pressure to surrender their independence."

Mr. Smith also formulated in his book, *The Right to Life,* the first "theology" of social security—that God intended nature to provide man's basic needs, but that man in his fallen state has progressively made this impossible. Society must assume this burden for those to whom other providence is denied. This may not be orthodox theology but it shows more understanding than the theology of the persons who arrogate to themselves the right to enjoy God's providence and deny it to others.

The process of decline from the humanist ideal is only just beginning. The church still has time to make its witness felt. In the next chapter we shall consider the more specific witness that the church can make.

Chapter IV

A Seven-Point Specific Witness

WE HAVE RECOGNIZED THE INADEQUACY OF THE church's present witness. We have looked at our past and present mistakes. We have seen the necessity of meeting the humanist challenge and our need both to learn from it and to illuminate it so that the good in its message is not lost. We should now be ready, with due recognition of how fumbling our answers must be, to formulate a more specific witness for the church in welfare matters. It will, of course, be a witness to principles and not to details, and must not suggest that the church knows best how to administer a difficult and complex program. But when the choice is between, say, more or less paternalism, or this or that major policy in which principle is involved, then the church should know its mind. It should be able to say, as it did of the projects of Juan de Vives in the sixteenth century, and as it did not in what happened in Newburgh, New York, in the twentieth, that a program is or is not in accordance with the Christian message.

Seven principles, admittedly overlapping, might be identified.

1. The church must stand on the side of *law as the basis for judgment,* not because the law is holy, or lawyers superior people, but because it is, in Reinhold Niebuhr's term, the best "proximate" solution. The judg-

ment of the saint or of the scientist inevitably leads to pride, which the church recognizes as the primary deadly sin.

What does this mean in practice? It means, that in public welfare, the church should stand on the side of those who are laboring to establish clear, honest, and fair legal criteria for relief. It means strengthening and approving certain good things that we have, such as a "fair hearing" procedure for the people to whom relief is denied. It means, in the current situation, going beyond our present law and urging the extension of the recipient's right from that of receiving relief to that of receiving at least a minimum amount of aid, sufficient for health and decency. This is something our present laws do not guarantee. It means being willing to recognize that the best law on earth is fallible; that a legal system will always grant relief to a few who appear not to deserve it, or to whom it may even do harm, but that it is unfair to deny to the many the dignity and the fairness of a legal system because a very few may abuse it.

At the same time it does not mean relieving men of responsibility. The law has the right to set conditions. If the law should require mothers with no preschool children to work, it has a right to do so. But the position must be clear. Either work is required or it is not. It must not be left up to the social worker, as moralist or as social scientist, or to public opinion in the individual case, to make such a decision for her. Again, a rule of law does not mean that those who cheat should not be punished, or that the state does not have the right to demand that recipients report changes in their circumstances.

What does it mean in other areas? It means a system of checks and balances, which the framers of our Constitution are said to have taken from Presbyterian policy, with its clear recognition of man's tendency to pride and to the control of his fellows. It means "due process" in the juvenile court—not the harshness of automatic justice, but the sureness, before the state intervenes in the life of a boy or girl, that such intervention is proper and not merely a disagreement between experts and the parents on how the child should be raised. It means being sure that even the humblest person knows his rights and is not overwhelmed by pressure brought on him by the rich, the learned, or those with authority. It means scrutinizing the growth of such concepts in criminology as "the indeterminate sentence," whereby, for all its rehabilatory and even merciful intent, a man may be held in subjection far longer than another who has committed the same offense.

It does not mean a lack of mercy, of recognition of those situations where the law needs tempering with a special understanding, such as were taken care of by the legal concept of equity. But it does mean an emphasis on man's right not to be subjected to the judgment of others, however expert or moral, until these have been accepted, by whatever imperfect and bungling ways we have, as the rule of all of us. And especially it means that he shall not be so subjected because he is humble or in need.

2. The church must stand on the side of man's *freedom of choice within the limits of the law.* This follows naturally from the first position. In practice it means being clear that man does not surrender his independence when he accepts aid or help, that he continues to make the normal decisions any man must make about his expenditures or his family, unless he is demonstrably incapable of so doing and the law would have to intervene anyway. This principle demands that relief be given in cash rather than in kind, or through meal tickets, surplus food, or old clothes.

The church's position here arises not only from its sense of how undesirable it is to subject a man to the tutelage of another, but from its understanding of how

God values human choice. God could have easily made man good, but he chose to give man freedom, even to choose the bad. Indeed, God made it a law of our being that man only grows and changes as he is free to make decisions. A man whose welfare grant is supervised in detail will not learn to be independent. As Lord Beveridge said in introducing England's system of family allowances, "If money is paid on any condition, it tends to bring that condition about; if it is paid or given on degrading conditions, sooner or later it degrades."

Of course this means taking risks. Some people will misuse their money and a few may need to be declared legally incompetent or even to be prosecuted for the protection of their families. But not to take the risk is to lose the opportunity for growth for the millions who are just as competent and just as incompetent as you or I in managing our affairs. And God takes many risks with man. Can His church fail to do the same, or must it always be over-careful for the sake of the errant few?

3. The church must assert its belief in the *possibility of redemption* for even the most unlikely. The church has too much experience of the working of God's surprising grace to accede too quickly to the proposition than any man cannot be redeemed. It may have to assert that at the moment it does not know how this can be done, or that redemption is possible only through a miraculous act of God. But at a time when social science seems to be turning to the negative diagnosis, and either stating that such people cannot be helped or that they can be so only if they are treated like children, the church is needed to keep alive the quest for ways to help them.

This has particular significance for an area in which the church is often engaged in social service itself—programs for dependent children who are away from home. In the past it was the church that condemned neglectful parents, and in its pride and presumption tried to bring up children apart from them. It was the humanists who insisted that the parent might be redeemable and that he still meant something to the child. Recently, and to the church's honor, the church institution has been exploring new ways of helping parents, whereas humanists have been turning to the coercive force of the law to sever children from parents who are judged incapable of taking help. This is perhaps the most positive witness that the church has as yet made, and it could be extended.

Deeply involved is the concept of forgiveness. Man is apt to repeat past behavior and without help he will often do so. But he is also sometimes capable of a "new start" under new conditions. The type of diagnosis that labels a man as psychopathic or ego deficient and then treats him accordingly offers him little chance of change. One of the surprising things about social-work practice is the discovery that so many apparently weak and worthless people have in them a capacity for growth and change. This faith the church must keep alive.

This is not an unrealistic faith in man or his "goodness." The church knows better than that. It is, rather, the assertion that in the end man is unknowable, that no human judgment can be final, and that God redeems even the most unlikely objects of his grace. And it means that failure to help another is cause for sorrow that one could not find the means to help, rather than an occasion for reprobation, despair, or recourse to force.

4. The church must insist on the *divorce of welfare from morality*. This is perhaps the most difficult witness it may be called on to make, for the church must be concerned with morality and it is almost expected to declare its constant opposition to sin. Yet the church is the only agency that can speak on the matter, for it alone knows what morality really is. It knows that morality cannot be forced, that it is, or should be, a response to love shown to man and not a means of purchasing love. It

knows that its Master's final judgments are not made on moralistic grounds but on the basis of man's need. Admittedly it has often been confused and has tried to place morality first as if morality were independent of the love that creates it. But this is not what its gospel says.

With this understanding the church must not only eschew morality as a source of judgment about who shall receive relief but cease trying to use man's need, his despair, or his helplessness as a means of inducing him to be moral. There is a double danger here. Not only do such methods fail to produce the kind of morality in which the church is interested, but they create a special class of vulnerable people of whom more is demanded than the church asks of itself. And this itself is presumption.

Let us look, for instance, at the recurrent problem of illegitimate children born to families who are receiving Aid to Dependent Children. No one pretends that this is a desirable situation. But repressive measures, in any case, cannot control the problem. It is a hard lesson for Protestant churches to learn what they might have learned from Geneva—that morality cannot be legislated. Crime—the commission of certain isolated acts against the good order of society—can to some extent be controlled or modified by a system of reward and punishment, although we are beginning to doubt how effective this usually is. But sin is a state and not an act, even though a specific act may be sinful. Sin is a condition vis-à-vis God, and is conquered by his love.

But suppose it were possible to reduce the number of such births by denying relief to those who had illegitimate children, or by sterilization, or by exposing the mothers to public shame? We would not have changed these women's basic morality or dealt with the problems that led them into temptation. Nor would we have brought them nearer God. Moreover, we would be dealing with only one tenth of all the illegitimate children who are born in the country today. Nine out of every ten illegitimate children are born to families who have the means to support them.

Have we the right to invoke this kind of sanction on a few, while we leave the greater part unscathed? Is this not pharisaism? To make relief depend on morality is to bribe people to be Christians, to force Christian morality on those who are our captives. This is not a Christian answer. Christ healed first and only afterward forgave a man's sins and hoped for a moral response from him.

Where relief is dependent on morality, it is all too often the innocent who suffer. This is particularly true in the Aid to Dependent Children program, in which attempts to punish the mother may leave the child without food or clothing. But there are some dangers in this argument. It assumes that it is right and proper in these situations for the mother to be denied help. Those who wish to do this often suggest removing children from their immoral parents and placing them in boarding homes or institutions. This is the cruelest solution that can be imagined, as anyone who works with "placed" children knows. It deprives the child in the name of justice and morality of a right even more important to a child than food and clothing.

There might be the possibility of conceiving a welfare law that was a direct stimulation to immorality—and if this were really so the church would have to object—but in most cases what really happens is that the immoral situation exists and the welfare law is merely trying to save what can be saved from it. Some welfare laws at the moment would appear, for instance, to make it easy for a man to desert his family with a more or less clear conscience, because he knows that they will be provided for. But this is like saying that having a fire department makes it less necessary to be careful about setting fires. It is not the welfare law that is faulty. Deserted children must be fed. The economic conditions that make such an alternative possible and the lack of efficient means of placing responsibility on the deserting father are what make desertion attractive. Nor is refusing to support those who are deserted the remedy. There is a dangerous kind of smugness which holds that because something is good or ought to happen, it is a reality and it should be taken for granted. One of the scandals of some of our welfare programs is that the grant is sometimes predicated on income which the family does not have. It only "ought" to have it. For instance, a family's income will be calculated to include contributions from an absent father or a son. Morally and even legally the family "ought" to have this money but in actual fact it does not. Meanwhile the family goes without, but the community's conscience is appeased.

There is, of course, one way in which welfare and morality can never be divorced. The law itself must be moral. It must show forth justice and loving-kindness. But a welfare law can never try to force people to be moral. To do so is incompatible with its essential purpose.

5. The church must advocate *adequate material welfare*. This means not only the provision of the means for a reasonably normal life but some security in it. Man must be free to choose the good, to be able to spend some of his thoughts and his energies on something outside himself. He must not be deliberately put into such anxiety about the very business of keeping alive that he has no time for God. It is true that God sometimes finds a person in such straits and helps him choose Him out of despair, but we are not asked to aid in this process. Indeed, the command to love one's neighbor as oneself would suggest the opposite. It is also very true that too much comfort or security can be as self-absorbing as poverty. This too should be avoided. But if human welfare

means anything, it means a life with some happiness, some joy, some participation in community life, and even perhaps some opportunity to contribute something in return. Without making the mistake of identifying the "good life" with material possessions, the church might want to consider what modern conveniences and recreational opportunities have become so much a part of everyone's life that to deny them to a welfare recipient sets him apart from his fellows.

To do this would mean abandoning forever the concept of "less eligibility," which is the effort to force people to become independent by making their lives, while dependent, gloomy and miserable. It would mean not using the threat of withdrawal of aid as a lever to frighten people into action. In actual fact there is evidence that just as many people have clung to relief because it was so hard to get, and because welfare workers were trying to hurry them off it, as have done so because relief was attractive. Delafield Smith, in discussing Jesus' exhortation to his disciples to take no thought for the morrow, has pointed out that in order for a man to dare to be independent he must have something to rely on. But man has destroyed the possibility of dependence on nature and the products of his labor and needs something to take its place. Those people who preach against the evils of security are often the ones who do not know what real insecurity means.

An adequate standard of relief does not mean luxury or indulgence. Indulgence is only another form of pity and is a form of paternalism and self-indulgence. But an adequate standard of relief does mean a reasonable standard of living. It does mean recognizing the importance of material things. We need to be honest with ourselves and recognize that no amount of counseling or social service, however essential to man's well-being, is a substitute for bread. Man needs both material and intangible help.

Jesus said, "fed me," "clothed me," not "counseled with me." (Matt. 25:35–46.)

6. The church must witness to the need for *stewardship rather than pity* or other forms of self-indulgent giving. The need for this understanding is most urgent in its own welfare programs, but it also has national aspects.

The church could, for instance, scrutinize carefully the motives behind the move to decentralize public welfare and "return it to the local community." Some of these motives may be good—a fear of centralized power, a need to adjust welfare to local conditions, a desire to bring it nearer to the people. But some of the motives stem from a need to judge or to patronize those in need, to deny the claims of a national conscience, or to protect local givers. Most home-grown programs are inadequate and most are moralistic. The church should be very sure, before it takes any stand against national taxation, that local relief would be adequate and that the motive behind it would be service and not control or personal satisfaction.

7. The church must be an advocate of *professional training and knowledge.* This may seem to contradict our insistence that the ultimate source of judgment must be law and not social science. But the objection is not to the sciences as a way of helping people. It is to their use to control them. The problem of helping those in distress is so complex and requires both knowledge and a trained self-discipline. One of the church's most dangerous illusions in its own welfare programs has been that good intentions, even piety, are enough. It has led it all too often into maintaining substandard and even harmful programs.

The social sciences, especially where they have become transformed into the science of working with people and not merely knowing about them, have much to give to the church. Despite some differences in philosophy, social workers have an understanding of the process of giving help, which many churches have never developed.

Redemption, or its secular counterpart, rehabilitation, is an internal and not an external matter. The real value of social services to a welfare program is not the "objectivity" with which relief is given. It is not knowing what would be good for this or that client. Nor is it wholly the "extras" that it can provide—medical care, or personal counseling. The major contribution of social work is the help given to people to thread their way through the complicated and difficult business of living on relief and to come to decisions about their future or themselves. Real help comes when relief is given in a dignified and understanding way so that the recipient can make use of it to grow and change if he wants to or come to terms with what has happened to him. This, rather than attempts to "rehabilitate" from the outside, is the true source of growth that relief sometimes makes possible. Some social workers do have knowledge of what will help, and are, by their very professional discipline, trained to work with empathy and a deep concern for their clients. Much of what they have learned can help the church understand the process whereby its basic convictions can be translated into practice.

But the church, in its turn, has much it can teach social workers. To insist that the persons who administer programs should have the best available training and knowledge, which the church insists on in its own sphere for its ministers, is not to approve wholeheartedly what is now taught nor accede to a philosophy the church cannot accept. The majority of schools of social work in this country are, it is true, at the moment committed to humanistic doctrines, and some are still wary of the church. Some are seeking a common ground with the church or have learned to respect religion as a factor in men's lives. Others, not necessarily church-sponsored or even always staffed by those who think in terms of the Christian message, are very much aware of what this message might contribute if the church were true to it. Today an increasing number of social-work students are graduates of seminaries or have theological interests.

The church has much to say that might illuminate the problem of those in need in our society. But if this illumination is to be conscious and consistent, it will need careful thought and a searching for principles. The seven outlined here are only a beginning.

Chapter V

The Church
and Its Own Welfare Programs

MOST CHURCH GROUPS MAINTAIN OR CONTRIBUTE TO some social service enterprise. Most of these are children's homes and homes for the aging, although some church groups are engaged in counseling services, probation work, adoption, foster family homes for children, nursing homes, homes for unwed mothers, and recreational activities. Overseas, church groups are providing a number of different services in connection with their mission activities, or are planning for refugees in this country. A recent estimate is that seven million people yearly receive help through church-related social agencies, but impressive as is this number, in terms of cost and man-hours of service the church's direct services are a small part of the welfare field.

These services are not for the most part, in the Protestant churches, a carry-over from the time when the church was the primary welfare agency. Usually they have come into existence when the church has seen a need that Government or community agencies have not met or are meeting too slowly. Sometimes there has been an additional motive—to care more adequately for one's own than secular agencies have been able to do. Both motives have led to the establishment of children's homes, which, as perhaps the most typical manifestation of the church's own social service, we will take throughout this chapter as the primary example of what happens in this field.

At the time when most children's homes were built, in the sixty years from 1860 to 1920, the plight of the dependent child was indeed serious. Often the only resource for him was the poor farm or workhouse—no place for a child—or apprenticeship to a master whose concern was primarily for the work that he might do. The church-sponsored orphanage was a vast improvement over other methods of care. It offered both a life designed as well as could be at that time for the needs of children and spiritual training which children in workhouses did not get.

There is a tendency, however, for something once established to continue to exist unchanged long after the need that brought it into being has ceased to operate. There is also a tendency for good motives to become perverted with the passage of time. Man needs always to rethink, with God's help, the purpose and form of his human institutions. Sin too often reveals itself in a good intention that is allowed gradually to be invaded by pride, sloth, or anger.

Children's homes today are not needed for the "orphan." Improved medical care now makes it unlikely that men and women should die in their child-rearing years. Not one child in thirty needing care away from home today does so because of the death of both his parents. On the other hand there has been a great increase in the number of children needing care because of the illness of their parents, and particularly because of their mental illness or neglect. Often it would take the wisdom of Solomon to decide what is sickness and what is sin on the part of the parents.

Again, children's homes are not today by any means the only way of caring successfully for children away from home, as was true when they were first established. The argument between people who believe in foster family care and those who believe in group care (children's institutions) is, let us be clear, a vain one. It seems abundantly clear that both types of care are needed. Nevertheless more children are today cared for in foster family homes than by children's institutions, and even more who would have formerly been put in orphanages are cared for in their own homes through public assistance programs. More important still is the evidence that some children are harmed by a kind of care not adapted to their needs. For instance, very small children may suffer real harm if they are reared in group care; as a result, some may be permanently retarded, physically, mentally, and emotionally.

Nor is the present church-sponsored children's home caring even largely for children of its own denomination. This may be true of some denominations with a very wide social "spread," but it is not true of the predominantly middle-class denominations.

In view of these facts we might well ask why a church continues to maintain a children's home and whether, if it does, the home might not need to be quite different from what it was thirty years ago. Would not the individual donor, who is in any case heavily taxed for state and national welfare purposes, be wiser to give what he still wishes to contribute to children's welfare to the Community or United Fund? Is the church's home perhaps a duplication, and even sometimes an inferior one, less skilled and less well supported than a public or community one?

There are, in fact, both good and bad reasons for the church's continued operation of a social service after the first immediate need for it has disappeared. There is, of course, the feeling that the church should "pull its weight" and contribute something to the general good. In many places, for instance, there are not enough facilities for children and any additional facilities are welcome. But this, although a worthy motive, is hardly the church's distinctive witness and is dangerous if not closely watched. Not only does it often tend to conceal from the public the deficiency in its service, but what began as the church doing its bit to help can so easily become a vested interest. Less good reasons for continuing a service are: tradition ("The church has always had a home"), the existence of costly buildings that must be used somehow, the fear of hurting the feelings of persons who have given their lives to some project that is not now needed. These reasons would be easily excusable if they did not sometimes hide deeper and more dangerous ones and if they did not sometimes hurt children by forcing them to use an unneeded or inappropriate service. But far more destructive to the church's witness are those services which continue in a spirit of antagonism to change or out of the church's pride in the products of its work.

Unfortunately, both reasons have operated to make some of the church's children's homes out of date and even harmful. Antagonism to change has been in part resistance to new knowledge, such as that some children genuinely need the kind of family life that a children's home cannot provide. It has been a denial of the well-documented fact that children reared exclusively in institutions, especially those who have never known family life, tend all too often to develop shallow, conforming, and inadequate characters—although there are notable exceptions. In part, it has been a superficial acceptance of conformity as the most desirable of all virtues to the neglect of more positive traits. Sometimes there has been resistance to the challenge presented by the broken family and to the humanist social worker's demand that these families be helped too. Sometimes there has been an inability to admit that the way to help these parents and children is not to condemn them for their past sins but to work with them. Some homes also cannot accept that the child belongs first and foremost to his parents and not to the home.

At this point antagonism to change merges with the church's institutional pride, its pointing to its "own" graduates, its counting of the ministers and successful businessmen its orphanages have produced. This is a particularly insidious form of pride, for it has often led churches to refuse to help or to dismiss the child who is most in need of help because he would not be a good advertisement for their service. Children have often been forced into a kind of care not suited to their needs. Sometimes they have even been taken away from their parents or their parents have been kept away from them because the church thinks it can do the parents' job better. Pride and traditionalism have also tended to create within the church a special class of docile "orphanage" children of whom a far higher moral code is demanded than of other children and whom the church patronizes through parties, gifts, and visitation. The church member who rejoices in the affection that homeless children show him when he visits his children's home is in effect starving children of true affection in order to indulge himself with a child's despair.

The church's children's home can, in fact, become the rallying point for all of its most comfortable heresies— for its moralism, its lack of forgiveness, and its preference for pity over Christian stewardship. If the church really believes that the rigid rules, the separation of the sexes, the life cut off from community contacts, and the excessive work schedule that are common in some of the more old-fashioned children's homes really produce the best kind of Christian character, it should prescribe such routines for every child, and condemn family life as too full of temptation to be permitted to exist. Only by considering the "orphanage child" as a separate class, a "they" and not a "we," could it avoid such a conclusion.

But there are also good and strong reasons for the continuance and evolution of a social service under church auspices. These come when the church finds for itself or adapts its service either to fulfilling a special need that the state or community have not touched, or where, although in a way "duplicating" other services, it does so in such a manner as to provide leadership in the field or witness to a particular and important truth.

The church does the first when it transforms its children's home into a treatment center for emotionally disturbed children, an expensive and difficult service that most states and communities are not able to undertake. It does so when it undertakes a difficult and numerically unrewarding service, such as adoption for hard-to-place children, or where it adds a counseling service in some area where it is lacking, such as with prisoners or refugees. In all these cases the church offers the service in the hope that later some secular agency will see its way to undertaking the service. The church will then be free to seek out and meet a new need.

The church is, by its very nature, particularly adapted to seek out such needs. It does not have to rely for support on tax funds or general solicitation, and it therefore does not have to meet the needs of everyone alike. It can select whom it can serve and in doing so awaken the conscience of the community to an unmet need. But the church must always be ready to give up what it is doing and seek out new and unrecognized needs. Once it clings to its own service, it ceases to lead and becomes again a cog in the wheel.

Alternatively, the church can perform a service in such a way that it witnesses to something that it believes to be important. This occurs when a church, for instance, accepts the challenge of the broken home and turns its children's home into a real family service in which the disaster that occasioned the family breakdown becomes not the death of the family but an opportunity for a new start in family relationships.

The rehabilitation of family life, although a challenge that the church can hardly ignore, is not the only possible witness. It is both expansive and difficult. A small church home that I studied recently has few facilities for service of this kind but is making a real witness in its loving care, not of the appealing child whom everyone loves to care for, but of the dull, the awkward, the backward "ugly duckling" for whom the competition of school and community are too much. This home is striving to help children "catch up" and take their place in society again. The Savior said, "Unto the least of these . . ." He did not mean to exalt the man or woman who finds it only too easy to love appealing little children. He meant to set us a hard task. He demanded that we love those we consider the least lovable or attractive.

The last few years have seen a great resurgence in church social service, particularly in the church children's home. In some areas and in some denominations, tradition, antagonism to change, and institutional pride have prevented any real witness or any real leadership, and the church's home has become a backwater. The majority, however, have shown such progress that the church children's home has become the fastest moving and most hopeful area in all social service. There are indications of the birth of a "third force" in modern social welfare supplementing and complementing the two that now dominate the field—public and community agencies. But there is still a long way to go before this force becomes strong enough to take its proper part in social services today.

Using the children's home again as the primary example, what might be required to make this dream come true?

Six things would seem to be needed. First, people need *knowledge* of what is really happening and what the church could do. Most of the men and women who work in the field know something about the changes and the discoveries of the past few years. But the people in the congregations, whose money supports the home or who elect Boards of Governors often know very little about it. They still envisage the problem as it was thirty years ago.

Such knowledge needs to go farther than the basic facts—the disappearance of the orphan and the development of alternative methods of care. It must include psychological facts such as the paramount importance to the child of his own family, so that it is far harder for a child who has a home, however inadequate, in the background to accept the church's care than it is for the orphan. Children coming to church homes today are confused, resentful, disturbed, and often hostile, lacking trust in themselves, in adults, and in Providence. These children need both expert care and tremendous understanding. We cannot expect them, at least at first, to be grateful for what we have done for them. Indeed, we have to let some of them hate us, for if they do not, they can hate only themselves or their God.

Secondly, churches must develop *humility*. This means recognizing that sometimes all the church can do is to help a child over a difficult period in his life instead of being all in all to him. It means being willing to learn, knowing that not even the church has the answers. Even more, it means not holding on to a service to which we can point with pride, which has showy buildings or in which there are a large number of children whom we can patronize or show off in public.

Thirdly, it means giving new meaning to *"loving our neighbor as ourselves."* It means not thinking of those the church serves as "they"—a special class of unfortunates or dependents—but as "we," "our" children, no different

from our own. Churches must want for these children
what they want for their own and try to get it for them.
They must not demand of them more than they would ask
of their own, either in behavior or work. Some children's
homes today demand of children standards of decorum or
a Sabbatarianism that the church has ceased to insist
upon in the lives of its congregation. If these things are
right, then let them be preached from the pulpit and
asked of all church members, not reserved for a special
group of children over whom the church happens to have
control. Many children's homes today still demand of the
"orphan" that he work far longer hours than a parent
would ask of his own children, and virtually to support
himself at an age when he can properly look to others to
care for him. Homes still exist in which a child goes to
school for a half day only, because he has to work on the
dairy farm or in the print shop to supply the home's finan-
cial needs.

Again, many homes today bring up boys and girls
strictly segregated from each other and with little or no
contact with the community. The children attend church
and school and live their entire lives within the institution's walls. This often results in a lack of any real prepa-
ration for living a normal life. The desire to shelter these
children from the outside world is, moreover, a denial of
the whole genius of the Reformation. Luther and Calvin
rejected the concept of the religious life apart from the
world. They insisted that the mature religious life was
lived in the world through one's daily vocation. Yet many
of their followers have rebuilt monasteries and convents
and called them children's homes. Those who have done
so lack the courage of the Reformers. They are afraid of
the world, afraid of life, and afraid of temptation.

The fourth thing needed is therefore *courage*. Courage
is needed to allow children to face and overcome temptation within limits. It takes courage to devise new ways of

meeting problems. Tradition is good. So is experience. But tradition based on fear and experience limited to the avoidance of problems is not worthy of the church. Nor can the church be content with the cautious introduction into its programs of ideas developed by other agencies. Other agencies need to look to the church for new ideas and new methods of making evident old truths. Church homes, for example, have experimented with "family living units" in which brothers and sisters and other boys and girls live together; with "off-campus" cottages for children who need group care but fewer routines than are found on the grounds of a home; with vacations at home; with work programs away from the home for children soon to be independent; with the adoption of older children; and above all, with the rehabilitation of family life. In some of these experiments they have led; in others, learned from secular agencies. Some have worked well; some have proved difficult. But all honor is due to the persons who had the courage to try them.

The fifth need is that for *excellence* in every department. One of the church's saddest illusions is that piety is sufficient. Sponsorship is no excuse for a home to have less than the very best both in skill and in facilities. Taking care of today's troubled children is not a job for the amateur. More harm has been done to children and to the church's reputation in welfare by this belief than by almost any other. Take, for example, the job of the "matron" or "houseparent," increasingly recognized as one of the most exacting in social service. It requires personal qualities of warmth, dedication, patience, and leadership, and in addition, trained knowledge in child psychology, group dynamics, and household management. These men and women meet twenty-four hours a day every known problem that can be presented by upset, lonely, growing children living together in groups. One of the greatest changes in group care in the last ten years has been the recognition of the importance of the child-care staff, and the field's responsibility to train them and give them support. Yet all too often it is assumed that the job can be done by any elderly Christian lady who needs charity herself. Houseparents are often miserably paid and expected to care for too many children to be able to give enough attention to the needs of each child. The same is true in other areas—in social casework, in the ministry, and in recreation, as well as in facilities. There is a persistent heresy that church care ought to be inexpensive, and many homes take more pride in low per capita cost than in the quality of their service.

The sixth point is the necessity for *self-sacrifice*. Good care for children is not cheap and if it is, it is not worth providing. Nor is the self-sacrifice demand confined to the expense of the program. The church has a mission in this field and cannot be content to care only for popular causes. It must be prepared to care for the unpopular and to give up a service when it becomes popular enough for support to be found elsewhere.

The church's moves to care for the elderly, so vigorous today, may well be a proving ground of its ability to provide a worth-while social service that witnesses to its faith. The need is certainly there. Whereas the primary interest of many churches is to take care of their own—and no one would deny them this right—the test will come in their willingness to develop a superior service for those.

Already decisions are being made on some very important issues. Are homes for the aging, for instance, to be confined to the middle classes, who can afford substantial entrance fees (as much, in some cases, as $15,000), or will they be open to those on old-age assistance as well as to those with savings? Are they to be confined to those to whom old age has come gracefully, or does the church have a redemptive mission to those who are difficult and unhappy? Can the homes guarantee life-time care or will they cease to care for the client when he becomes bed-ridden or needs nursing care? Are those who run them skilled in meeting the needs of the aging—a new and exciting field of study in which there are few experts—or are old folks' homes to be just another amateur effort by kindly churchmen who will soon fall behind the rest of the world? Are homes to be built as real centers of service or as memorials to the charity of the church? This one question may decide whether older persons are engaged in the community, perhaps in smaller units, or isolated from the community in some stately rural mansion.

There are signs of forward thinking among the persons who are developing this new service. But, as in all fields of social service, the church needs to think through its witness, to do something better than, or different from, that which the state or the community can do, to know itself not as just another charitable society but one whose message is so amazing and yet so relevant that if put into practice it cannot but illumine the world.

Chapter VI

The Theology of Personal Helping

MANY PEOPLE IN A CHURCH ARE INVOLVED IN HELP-
ing others, as members of a social service committee, or
personally, or, in increasing numbers, as board members
or as paid or volunteer workers in the church's own social
services. Rather few of these people have given much
thought to what helping another involves. Helping seems
to be something that we do "out of the goodness of our
hearts." If the person one helps is ungrateful, misuses or
wastes the gift, or if he seems none the better for our
help as soon as our back is turned, then we are disap-
pointed in him. We label him as undeserving or resolve
that next time we will be more careful to tie strings to our
giving, if indeed we give at all.

These are bitter experiences and we have all had them.
They are apt to color not only our personal giving but
our whole concept of welfare. Even our country's foreign
policy has been affected by such feelings, for quite clearly
some countries have been ungrateful or have wasted
American help. Yet there is a simple truth which we sometimes forget. Helping is a two-way process, involving both
giver and recipient, and sometimes what goes wrong with
helping is as attributable to the giver as to the recipient
of aid.

We can understand this a little if we consider what

taking and giving help means. There is, of course, a kind of giving that is immediate, essential, and given without thought of the future—the life belt thrown to the drowning man or help in putting out a fire. There is also help that is casual and not significant, such as giving the neighbor's car a push or helping a blind man across the street. But most of the help in which we are interested looks to the future. It is concerned with change on the part of the person receiving it, with his doing something about his problem. Perhaps with our help he can become independent, get an education, or straighten out his finances, his marriage, or his health. We give in the hope that the recipient will respond to our helping by making a commitment to something new.

Now we in the church know how difficult it is to respond even to the most amazing act of love that the world has ever known. We know how hard it is to commit ourselves to change. We know that change demands repentance, the recognition that there is something wrong with our lives. We know that it demands submission, letting God know us and have power in our lives. We know that it demands faith, a giving up of the familiar in the hope of something better that as yet we do not know. We know that we cannot always consciously control our choice. "For I do not do the good I want, but the evil I do not want is what I do." (Rom. 7:19.) It is obvious to Christians that all these things are involved in receiving help from God. What is not so clear is that to take meaningful help from another person involves essentially the same process. To take help from anyone involves recognizing that something is wrong, telling someone else about it, and letting the person into one's life and one's plans, however partially, and giving up the known, however uncomfortable, for something as yet not experienced. It is, in fact, more difficult to take help from another human being than it is to take help from God. God always respects the integrity of his creatures, but the man who takes help from another can never be sure that the other will not subtly use the power that helping gives over another.

Is it surprising then that some people, however much they need help, will do almost anything to avoid taking help that really counts? Is it surprising that some people seem ungrateful or that they demand help as a "right" or on their own terms? "Give me a check and leave me alone." Is it surprising that some of them seem to us hypocritical, agreeing with everything we say while we are there, but later rejecting our help and our advice? One of the best ways of not taking help from God, as many ministers could testify, is to go to church every Sunday, sing all the hymns, go through all the motions, and never actually listen to God's disturbing demand.

How can we help people who are afraid of taking help? It is not a matter of trying to explain to them what would be good for them. Most of them know that already. What they do not know is how to accept help, to want it, not to be frightened of it. For what holds people back from being able to take help is basically fear—fear of the unknown, fear of trusting people, fear of not being able to live up to expectations, fear of being dominated or obligated to others, fear of being known for what they are. Fear is rarely overcome by argument or persuasion, far less by punishment or shaming. The attempt to force people to take help is perhaps better than washing our hands of them, but it is still an act that comes from our own frustration. It is not loving our neighbor as ourselves, and is, in any case, highly inefficient, forestalling forever real help and real change.

The need to discover ways of really helping people becomes then not only a moral but a pragmatic necessity. It is not only a matter of how we *ought* to behave as Christians toward those we are helping, but how we *must*

behave toward them if real help is to be possible and our
charity is not to be wasted. And, as so often in such matters, the Bible gives us the answer. Perfect love casts out
fear. But this, like most Biblical truths, is easier to say
than to put into practice.

Perhaps the first thing to understand is that no man
can "give" help to another. All we can do is to make it
possible for another to use the help we offer. The final
choice will always be the recipient's. He must choose to
use help. And this "choice"—I put the word in quotes
advisedly—is an intensely personal matter, akin to what
the church means by the word "commitment." It means
putting the whole of oneself into the overcoming of fear,
into the resolution to get well, to do better, to find a way
out of one's troubles.

There is plenty of evidence of the importance of this
kind of choice in every helping profession. Doctors know
the patient for whom "everything is done" but who, unaccountably, fails to get well, and conversely, the "hopeless case" whose will to live pulls him through. Ministers
know that no amount of argument or persuasion makes a
man a believer. Some make this choice and some will not,
because of something within themselves. Social workers
know the client who does something with help that is
offered and the one in apparently the same circumstances
who cannot. All the helping professions know that this
difference cannot be ascribed to better heredity, better
environment, or some innate "superiority." It is often the
most unlikely kind of person who shows this strength.

Two things immediately become clear about this kind
of "choice." First, it is not the kind of choice that someone else can make for one, or even persuade one or urge
one to make. It has to be one's own decision. And secondly, it has little in common with what we usually mean
by "choice," the rational choosing between two alterna-
tives. Man does not choose, in the ordinary sense of the

word, between God and the devil. He does not toss a coin to see which he will follow. Either he commits himself to God or he does not. In the same manner a man's essential choice in this matter of getting help is not, "Shall I do this or that?" but "Shall I or shall I not allow myself to change?"

The nature of this choice is frequently misunderstood not only by the public but by those who advocate and even practice "permissive" or "nondirective" methods of helping. Social work and the ministry have as a result sometimes been thought starry-eyed and impractical. To recognize that man must make this one essential kind of choice before he can be helped is one thing and is an intensely practical matter. If this choice is not made, the help a man receives will be of no use to him. It is quite another thing to argue that man must be free to make all sorts of lesser decisions, even those which are illegal or immoral, just because he ought to be free to choose. This is both unethical and silly. A prisoner in jail cannot decide where he will live, what he will wear or eat or do, but he can make the one choice that matters. He can decide what he will do with his imprisonment. He can use it to learn a new trade or to rethink his values. He can spend his time trying to escape. He can become embittered, or worse, escape into daydreaming and self-justification.

We do not have very far to go to see that this is the kind of choice that God demands of us. He does not force us to choose one way or the other, but he does make it possible for us to make a positive choice by taking away our fear. Our problem, as human helpers, is to find ways in which we too can make it possible for people to make this kind of positive choice.

We in the church, although it hurts sometimes to admit it, have much to learn here from the secular helping professions that have grown up in this century. And these professions do know something of the conditions that are necessary before the recipient of help can make real use of it. It should not surprise us that what they have discovered should in some way mirror a divine process. In fact we would be surprised if what we believe to be the Christian position should not also prove to be the most effective. Christianity is not an "ideal" but a very real understanding of things as they are.

Perhaps the first thing to realize is that all real helping takes place within a relationship. It is the helped person's trust in the helper that makes it possible for him to risk changes in himself. But this relationship needs to be understood. It is not a matter of liking, admiring, or even "getting along well with" the other person. The most helpful relationships are not always smooth ones. But the relationship does have certain characteristics that we can examine.

First of all, since it must be a relationship in which the helped person is free to make whatever ultimate choice he wishes, both positive and negative choices must be considered and weighed. It may sound paradoxical to say, but *a positive choice is possible only where the opposite choice is also allowed.*

Intellectually this may not be too hard to see. Man cannot choose to be good unless he can also choose to be bad. If God had compelled man to be good, he would not be good at all. Again, man cannot choose to live fully unless he can also choose (or accept) death. Nothing is gained without risk, and to say "Yes" sincerely always means that I could have said "No." All of us recognize this when we speak slightingly of the "Yes man."

But this principle is terribly hard to put into practice. We so much want the man we are helping to make one decision and not the other, to choose the right and not the wrong, growth and not regression. Even to recognize the possibility that he may choose wrongly seems like treason to us. We work for a church deeply committed to the overcoming of sin. How can we freely tell a man that he is free to sin?

And yet he cannot choose to get well unless he can choose to be ill. He cannot be pushed, forced, or even gently manipulated into choosing to get well if we want him to make a real decision. This is the mistake that so many churches, courts, and schools make time and time again. We try to "make" people good and in doing so make it impossible for them to be so.

Perhaps the point can be made clearer by exploring what is meant here by the opposite, or negative, choice. This is not simply a failure to choose the good. Such failures occur when we try to *make* someone into something that he has not chosen to be and he fails to live up to expectations. They are utterly defeating. But there is always a negative choice which has something of triumph about it. It is the determination not to do what is expected of one, not to have anything to do with this kind of help. It is the decision to "go it alone," to "take the consequences." Man, if he is to be helped, must always be free to choose this kind of rebellion, even to "curse God, and die" (Job 2:9). God takes this risk with us, and we have to take it with others, all the more because our knowledge of the good is imperfect and what may be good for us may not be good for another. Even if we are sure of the good, we must still take the risk. The person who makes the wrong choice is much closer to help than he who makes no choice at all, who evades the problem, or fears to go either way. This, of course, reinforces the knowledge that the choice must be made by the person helped. It can neither be made nor even too passionately desired by the helper.

Secondly, the helping relationship must be one in which the helped person's *anger, doubts, fears, and despairs can be expressed without fear of blame or loss of face*. These are the feelings that make it hard for a person to use help constructively. One cannot get help with these feelings, some fashionable preachers to the contrary, by pretending that they are not there. Yet the expression of negative feelings is something that most of us find it very hard to allow. We want to keep our helping on a positive, reassuring, and cheerful basis. But when we do so, we in effect deny the helped person's problem. We pretend that it is not there instead of helping him come to grips with it. It is not without significance that Jesus' first act on accepting his calling was to face up to temptation, identify it, and overcome it. He did not pretend it did not exist.

This in turn means that a helping relationship cannot be one of superior and inferior, saint and sinner, wise and foolish, judge and judged, or even their modern equivalent, adjusted and unadjusted. The differences may objectively be present, or society may have given one of the pair responsibility to act as if there was a difference by appointing him judge or teacher. But as helper and helped struggle together to understand, to come to a point where the helped person makes his decision to change or not to change, they must struggle as equals, either of whom could have felt and thought like the other. This is what we mean when we use glib phrases such as "respect for human dignity" and "accepting people as they are." Both helper and helped are, for all their difference, fallible and imperfect creatures who, if not capable of the particular weaknesses in question, are capable of many others.

Four other conditions that make possible the commitment to change more or less follow from these three.

First, *the relationship must be centered entirely on the interests of the person served.* It cannot be centered in the helper's need to be liked, to control, or even to satisfy his own conscience. It cannot *immediately* be centered on any other good, such as the good of society, the honor of the church, public morality, justice or fair play; although once real help is given, these generally will be added to it. It is a common mistake to try to kill two birds with one stone and thereby miss them both. The helped person's need is antecedent. It must come first. If it does not, we are using him as a tool, not loving him as ourselves.

Secondly, *it must deal with real things.* Helping must always deal with real things, however unpleasant. A doctor who refused to consider cancer of the anus because he was afraid of cancer or preferred to ignore the bathroom would be no doctor at all. In the same way, help with other kinds of problems must deal with what is really there. It must struggle with real sorrow, real hate, real sin, and real despair. It cannot take refuge in false reassurance, polite evasions, or "pie in the sky." Just as Jesus, who remains the supreme example of empathy, shared with us all the unpleasant things of life—hunger, thirst, temptation, and even the sense of being cut off from his God—just as he "descended into hell," so the man who would really extend help must be prepared to face hell with the people he helps. This is why real helping can be so utterly exhausting.

In the third place, the relationship must be based on faith in *a belief that man can be helped,* however wayward he may seem. It is true that at any one moment we may not be able to help him. Sometimes, too, man's first efforts at change seem to go in the wrong direction and may even seem dreadful to us. But love "bears all things, believes all things, hopes all things, endures all things" (I Cor. 13:7), not only because patience and long-suffering are virtues, but because man, to be helped, needs the strength of another who will not fail him in distress. The helper must not force help on others when they are not ready for it. But he is always there to help them. He understands their blundering attempts to change and he forgives them not seven times but seventy times seven.

Finally, the relationship must be based on *humility*. Ultimately the helping person does not know what is right for another. He is lucky indeed if he knows it for himself. He does not have to face what the helped person is facing. It is all too easy to face temptations at second-hand. No one can know what another's temptations are really like. Even more important is the fact that the helping person cannot and ought not to try to acquire the kind of knowledge about people that claims to know all about them. Even to assert that someday this knowledge may be acquired is to deny the divine in man. It reduces him to the status of a complicated machine or a superior animal. The true helper knows that the more he studies man the less he knows about him.

Individual helping, then, as all helping, requires, first and foremost, self-discipline. This is why there are professional schools of social work and of other professions for people who want to make a career of helping. In these schools knowledge is often less important than the student's ability to acquire the kind of self-discipline that enables him really to help another. But since a great deal of the helping in the world must be done by people who do not make a career of it, people need to discover ways to find self-discipline for themselves. Many could find such a way in what the gospel teaches us about God and man. Here one can learn to know what man is, both in his frailty and in his glory, and to know ourselves no different. Out of such a study might come three questions the would-be helper might properly ask himself.

Do I really want to help? Do I want to put myself truly at the service of another? Or do I in my heart of hearts really want to be thanked, to control, or to ease my own conscience? Those who cannot honestly say that they want to serve others in a personal way would perhaps be wiser to confine their helping to the giving of money to a cause in which someone else will do the helping. God gives each

of us different talents. One man may have a gift for helping and another serve in quite a different way.

Am I strong enough to help? Those who think that
helping others, either professionally or as a volunteer, is
an easy and perhaps even an unmanly occupation, suitable
perhaps for a minister or a woman with time on her
hands, know little about what helping demands. True
helping calls for a great deal of courage. It takes strength
to face reality, to risk anger, even to court it, to strip the
polite veils from sorrow, to allow those you help to make
mistakes, to endure their doubts and despair. It takes courage not to disarm people, minimizing their troubles in
order to keep one's relationship with them pleasant and
devoid of deep meaning.

Am I meek enough to help? The helping person needs
to be strong, but he must also be humble. Love does not
insist on its own way. It does not demand exclusive rights
to help others and it recognizes that sometimes the help
it can give is very small. The helper must be able to say
sincerely, "There, but for the grace of God, go I."

This book ends, then, as it began: with a plea for a
more theological approach to the problems of help and
welfare. In its witness in welfare in general, in the operation of its own social programs, and in the personal helping of its members, the church's witness must be to the
essentials of its faith. Because this faith is the truth, it
will also be found practical. The fact that the church's
faith may lead it to positions that are not popular or
easily understood is no reason to try to modify that faith.
Christians all too easily identify what they believe with
tradition or with prevailing cultural, economic, and philo-
sophical ideas of their time. There can be no "buts" about
the Christian gospel. A letter in a church paper recently
contained the words: "To turn the other cheek is all very
well, but . . ." In welfare, as in all other concerns, the
church's business is not to decide which of its principles

can be accepted and which "are all very well, but . . ."
The church is called to act in accord with all its principles and to have faith that they will prove what we know
them to be, true in every sense of the word.

That there is risk in this proposal, no Christian would
deny. But this is the risk which the Christian is called
on to undertake, in the unshakable knowledge that the
truth will prevail.

Questions for Study and Discussion

Chapter I

1. Do you see the church as (*a*) unconcerned with, (*b*) as a rival to, or (*c*) as a stimulator and critic of modern welfare programs? How does your answer reflect your belief in what the church really is? How does your own church measure up to this concept?

2. What is lacking most in the present witness of the church with regard to welfare programs? Would an exhortation to brotherly love be a sufficient witness? If not, why not?

3. Consider any statements you may have made in public or in private about welfare programs in your community or your state. To what extent were these based on (*a*) knowledge of what was really happening and (*b*) a thoughtful appraisal of man's relationship to God and to his fellow creatures?

Chapter II

1. Consider your own giving, or the giving of your church. How much of it is really stewardship? How much do you, or does your church, take pride in what is given? How much gratitude do you (or does your church) expect?

2. The discussions of the commandment "Honor thy father and thy mother" in Luther's Large Catechism and in the Westminster Larger Catechism (Questions 123–132)

81

speak of "our several relations, as inferiors, superiors, or equals." How do the "great heresies of the church regarding welfare" relate to these ideas? What do they imply about the relationship between the rich and the poor? How much are they typical of relationships today? How do you reconcile them with your belief in man's common sinfulness?

3. A man once said to Thomas Chalmers that if you give a man a coat he will be able to come to church. Chalmers replied that if you can get him to come to church, he will get himself a coat. Who was the more realistic? The more charitable?

Chapter III

1. In what way did the depression of 1929–1937 contribute to our understanding of human need? To what extent have we forgotten its lessons?

2. What kind of position would make you most likely to develop independence and self-reliance: (a) a job in which you were relatively secure, well treated, and trusted or (b) a job in which you were miserably underpaid, supervised in what you did, and generally despised? Which kind of job would give you the more confidence to go on to better things? What does your answer have to do with welfare policies today?

3. Consider the seven deadly sins, as named by the ancient church—gluttony, anger, lust, sloth, envy, avarice, and pride. Which has the Protestant Church condemned most often, and which largely ignored? Which did Jesus condemn most commonly?

Chapter IV

Consider the Christian principles involved in the following actions. What might be the church's stand on these matters? On some, there may be genuine disagreement.

1. A welfare worker makes a practice of checking with the grocery store. When she finds that Mrs. A buys only essentials, whereas most of her clients include some "frivolities" such as candy for the children, she tells Mrs. A that she is "very pleased with her."

2. A state legislature decides that old people need at least $65 a month. In determining how much needs to be added to an applicant's present income, welfare workers are permitted to set aside $10 of this for "special needs of the aged," including recreation, newspapers, and a telephone.

3. A young couple, much preoccupied with their own marital problem, fail to give their children proper care. On the basis of a court psychiatrist's evaluation that the couple "have a poor potential for parenthood" the child welfare agency does not ask the couple to contribute toward their children's support and discourages visiting, in the hope that the parents will drop out of the picture and the agency obtain authorization to place the children for adoption with a substantial and stable family.

Chapter V

1. If you visit a children's home and the children cling to you, are you (a) proud of what you can give them or (b) penitent because the children are not getting enough affection from people who should mean more to them?

2. If you have a group in the church interested in your children's home, would it be best employed: (a) in interpreting the home's program to the congregation? (b) in planning parties for the home's children? (c) in "adopting" particular children who show promise and buying clothes and gifts for them?

3. If your church supports a home for the aging, does the home (a) require a large entrance fee? require that a resident turn over his savings to the home? (b) guarantee lifetime care? (c) encourage residents to take part in activities outside the home?

Chapter VI

1. Consider some time in your own life in which you have asked for help. What were your feelings? How hard was it to bring yourself to ask for help?

2. Why is a Pollyannalike, bright, and cheerful social worker sometimes less effective than a quiet, less outgoing type?

3. A refugee family that was brought to this country is helped by a local church. A house is secured and furnished, and the father is found a well-paying job. Nevertheless, at the end of the year the family moves to another community and the father to a job that pays a little less. What might such a story tell about the church that helped them in the first place?